ILLUSTRATED HISTORY OF
BASEBALL

ILLUSTRATED HISTORY OF
BASEBALL

ALEX CHADWICK

CHARTWELL
BOOKS, INC.

Published by
CHARTWELL BOOKS
a division of Book Sales, Inc.
Raritan Center
114 Northfield Avenue
Edison, New Jersey 08818

Produced by
Brompton Books Corp.
15 Sherwood Place
Greenwich, Connecticut 06830

ISBN 0-7858-0223-1

Printed in China

PAGE 1: *The Sultan of Swat, Babe Ruth, poses with slugger Jimmie Foxx of the Athletics in 1934.*

PRECEDING PAGES: *Pirate Phil Garner nails Steve Garvey of the Dodgers and goes for two in a 1980 game.*

THESE PAGES: *Yankees pitcher Whitey Ford puts one past Reds pitcher Jim O'Toole in game four of the 1961 World Series. Catching for the Yankees is Elston Howard, and Augie Donatelli is the umpire. The Yankees went on to win the Series four games to one and Ford was named Series MVP.*

Contents

Introduction

Baseball, it can sometimes be forgotten, is a game to be played with a bat, a ball, some gloves, a field, and a group of people. (And it is not just chauvinistic guilt that substitutes 'people' for 'males': females of all ages are now involved with baseball.) In all the hullabaloo surrounding baseball these days – whether it arises from agents seeking better contracts or TV announcing spectacles or writers paying their self-conscious tributes to the 'meaning' of the game – it is easy to forget how fundamentally simple the game can still be. In a pinch, any half-round object will do, a stick can replace a Louisville Slugger, gloves are not really necessary, and a sandy beach can replace a grassy field: only the people, it turns out, are necessary. But it must be said that playing the game always comes first – no matter where, or with what, or how well.

And then comes watching a live game: any real game, played by people of whatever age or sex or skill. Better a game between Peewee Leaguers, with the score 12-0 and the losing pitchers yet to have given up a fair hit, than settling down with the rest of the couch potatoes to view the World Series. There might be some arguments on that one. . . . So let's concede: failing a live game, a televised game will do.

But eventually the stadium lights go out, the field is empty, and everyone must go home. And then, but only then, out come the books and articles on baseball. What a library they now make up! Works of fiction and non-fiction, turgid social history and sensitive poetry, ribald novels and dry analyses, doctoral dissertations and sports-mag valentines – the numbers of words and volumes of text inspired by baseball now defy counting.

Why, then, another? Well, for one reason, true lovers of the game never tire of reading the same old stories. Beyond that, it remains true that pictures, if worth not a thousand words, are worth a special kind of words. Words can recount the bare bones of the history of the game, but they cannot fully capture the human aspect. Pictures, however, can take us back through time and remind us of, or introduce us to, the roots and trunk and spreading limbs and glorious leaves of the great elm that is truly America's national pastime.

Some words, admittedly, do succeed at this – words by the truly great writers and poets. But these are few and far between, even considering the many fine words that have been written to convey the game of baseball. And the fact remains that there is some ineffable appeal, literally a wordless drama, that is expressed by a collection of pictures of baseball. So it is through pictures, our substitutes for the actual experience, that we feel most attuned to the ongoing song of baseball. Donald Hall, a fine poet and, need it be said, an appreciator of baseball, puts it well when he says: 'It is by baseball, and not by other American sports, that our memories bronze themselves. Other sports change too fast, rise with the highrise, mutate for mutability, modify to modernize. By baseball we join hands with the long line of forefathers and with the dead.'

To turn through and examine a book such as this is to join hands with the 'forefathers' of the game. But Hall, writing in an elegiac mood, would be the first to admit that many people are primarily attracted to the living phase of the game – the active players, the ongoing season. And so a true history of the game such as the book that follows has plenty for all – text and pictures for those who never tire of staring hard at the faces and positionings of the old-time players, and for those who cannot see enough of or read enough about their latest heroes.

It is all here – players, teams, managers (even some owners and commissioners), crucial games, songs, sculpture, minor and youth leagues, foreign teams, forgotten heroes and national idols. From the oldest games to the latest season, here is an illustrated history of baseball.

CHAPTER ONE

Children's Game to National Pastime

The transformation of baseball from a children's game into America's national pastime stands out as one of the great social phenomena of the nineteenth century. In less than 50 years the game evolved from an amusement of the elite to a commercial sport of such enduring popularity that over 100 years after the formation of the first professional league in America, 80 million spectators – the greatest number to attend any spectator sport in America in 1986 – attended major league, minor league and college games. This number of fans is four times greater than the population of the United States at the time of baseball's inception.

Although baseball as we know it was shaped in its essentials in New York City in the mid-1840s, no documentation or delving into antiquity can ever completely fathom the origins of games with balls and bats. The first written records of such games come to us from ancient Egypt, where diversions with balls and bats were grounded in fertility rituals and sometimes played by scantily-clad women; mosaics from a 2000-year-old Carthaginian nobleman's home depict an activity very much like baseball, and it is not hard to imagine cave men passing time by hitting rocks with clubs. Sticks and projectiles were, after all, the stock in trade of early professional hunters.

Most historians believe that ball playing, immensely popular and still tied to fertility rituals and the cycles of the seasons, reached Europe from Egypt, transmitted by the expanding Muslim empire. By the time Islam retreated from Europe, ball games had surfaced in Christian ceremonies from Austria to France. During the Middle Ages, the French Cathedral of Rheims wound up its Easter celebrations with widely anticipated ball games in which the ball was kicked or swatted with a stick.

TOP: *Bat-and-ball games were played in medieval England, as depicted in this thirteenth-century manuscript.*

ABOVE: *A popular American book of 1834,* The Book of Sports, *shows boys playing baseball on Boston Common.*

TOP RIGHT: *Henry Chadwick, an English-born journalist, is one of baseball's true 'founding fathers' because of his devotion to promoting and improving the game.*

PRECEDING PAGES: *This well-known Currier & Ives lithograph depicts what is now believed to be a game played on 3 August 1865 between the New York Mutuals and the Brooklyn Atlantics.*

When ball games crossed the Channel to England the dominant form became stoolball, a game in which a pitcher tried to hit an upturned stool with a ball before a batter could hit it away. As early as 1330 some English clerics were suggesting that Easter ball games be divorced from the churchyard, and they did move rapidly into the English countryside, where milkmaids added more stools, or 'bases,' which had to be rounded if the batter succeeded in striking the ball. The game remained curiously true to its origins as fertility ritual for some time after it left the churchyard, for it was played by both sexes and retained its status as a sanctioned occasion for discreet love-making.

American baseball's immediate precursor, rounders, was created with the implementation of the rule that a base runner could be put out by being hit with a thrown ball. English schoolboys planted posts in the ground to replace the stools and the game, now primarily an activity of children, was widely known as 'goal ball' or 'base ball' at least as early as 1700. *A Pretty Little Picture Book,* published in London in 1744 and in Boston beginning in 1762, contained an illus-

tration and rhyme captioned 'Base Ball.' *The Book of Sports,* published in 1834, included illustrations and instructions on how to play 'base ball.' By then baseball in America was becoming, like cricket, a favorite diversion of young men as well as of boys. It was in gentlemens' clubs of the eastern cities that the game was shaped into a form that by the 1840s would have been recognizable to a visitor from the twentieth century.

Still many variations and inconsistencies remained, the rules often changing from club to club. Students of the early history of the game agree that it was a committee appointed by the Knickerbocker Base Ball Club of New York City, one of the first of the gentlemens' clubs organized to play baseball, that proposed a set of rules that systematized the game. These rules, adopted by the Knickerbockers on 23 September 1845, may be regarded as the 'founding' of modern baseball if any one event can be said to so qualify. One of the most important rules adopted by the Knickerbockers was that a player could be tagged or forced out but not thrown at. This provision forever separated baseball from the very popular 'Massachusetts game' or 'town ball,' versions of which persisted long enough for Ty Cobb to recall having played them in his youth.

The best known of the early games played under the new rules was one between the Knickerbockers and the so-called New York Nine, played at Hoboken, New Jersey, on 19 June 1846. The Knickerbockers lost, 21-3, and had to pay for the victors' dinner; an umpire fined one of their players six cents for swearing. Despite such ungentlemanly behavior, baseball was becoming a great success among the gentry and the 'New York Game' soon became the basis for competition.

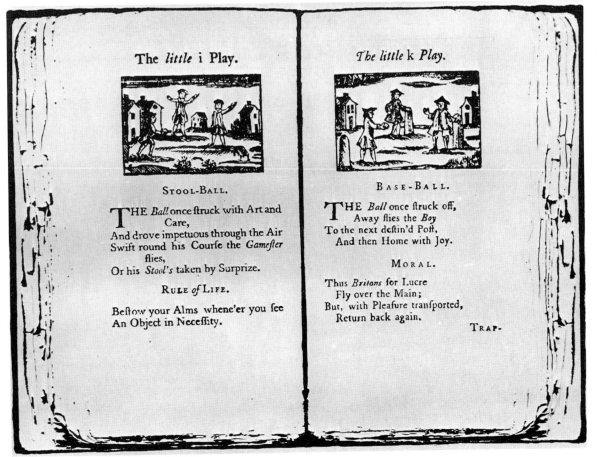

The *little* i Play.

STOOL-BALL.

THE *Ball* once ftruck with Art and
    Care,
And drove impetuous through the Air
Swift round his Courfe the *Gamefter*
    flies,
Or his *Stool's* taken by Surprize.

RULE of LIFE.

Beftow your Alms whene'er you fee
An Object in Neceffity.

The *little* k Play.

BASE-BALL.

THE *Ball* once ftruck off,
    Away flies the *Boy*
To the next deftin'd Poft,
    And then Home with Joy.

MORAL.

Thus *Britons* for Lucre
    Fly over the Main;
But, with Pleafure tranfported,
    Return back again.

TRAP-

ABOVE: *These mature-looking
gentlemen are some of the
New York Knickerbockers, the
first baseball team known to
play by rules close to modern
rules. Center rear is
Alexander Cartwright, often
credited with singlehandedly
drawing up these rules; it is
now known that, although he
was an active promoter of the
Knickerbockers and early
baseball, the rules were drawn
up by a committee of
Knickerbockers.*

LEFT: *One of the prime
exhibits for the case that
baseball long preceded Abner
Doubleday, who some claim
invented baseball, is a book
published in London in 1744,
A Pretty Little Picture
Book. Among the various
children's games described are
'stool-ball' and 'base-ball,'
predecessors of such games as
rounders, cricket, and
baseball.*

RIGHT: *The Brooklyn Excelsiors, pictured here in 1860, were the first team to go 'on tour,' to upstate New York. Third from the left is famed pitcher Jim Creighton; legend has it that he died from injuries caused by a mighty swing he took.*

BELOW: *Although baseball was played in the South before the Civil War, the game became truly popular there after Confederate soldiers watched Union prisoners playing, as pictured here at a prison in Salisbury, North Carolina, in 1862.*

OPPOSITE TOP: *A typical amateur team of the post-Civil War era was the Morrisania Unions of New York City. Note the size of the bat.*

Newspapers had begun reporting on the games as early as 1845; soon magazines were reporting on and depicting the game in their columns. By the 1850s contemporary commentators were describing the phenomenal popularity of the spectator sport as a national mania. Henry Chadwick, known as the 'Father of the Game' for his 50 years of baseball sportswriting and promotion, was publishing box scores (modelled after cricket scores) by the time the first baseball league was formed in 1858.

On 10 March 1858, 25 of the more than 100 clubs playing the New York Game in the Northeast met to form the National Association of Base-Ball Players, a strictly amateur organization. By 1860 the Association numbered 60 clubs and attracted considerable attention as its members battled for the championship of the United States. By now the maturing of the game was forcing major changes in the Knickerbocker rules that had served with slight modifications over the years. One of the Association's first and most significant alterations was to create a nine-inning game (The Knickerbocker game was won by first team to score 21 runs). In 1863 the Association began calling balls on batters, and in 1867, under the guise of preserving the gentlemanly nature of the game, the Association began baseball's long, unfortunate tradition of discrimination by formally barring blacks and any clubs they played on.

In 1858, the first year of the Association, Harry Wright, a jeweler's apprentice who happened to be a cricket professional, was invited to join the Knickerbockers to help them battle the Brooklyn Athletics; by 1860 James P Creighton – generally considered the first professional player – was being paid sub rosa to pitch for the Excelsiors of Brooklyn. Also in 1858, the first admission in the history of baseball – 50 cents – was charged at an All-Star game between Brooklyn and Manhattan teams. By 1862 the New York Mutuals and the Atlantics were splitting the gate after expenses from a 10-cent admission.

ABOVE: *Harry Wright was born in England and played cricket in America before switching to baseball. He played and managed from 1858 to 1893.*

RIGHT: *Pictured here are 'the first nine' of the Cincinnati Red Stockings, the team that in 1869 was the first to announce publicly that it was paying all its players. This commenced the professionalization of baseball, and the Red Stockings' dominance of other teams inspired others to follow suit.*

FIRST THE NINE.

ABOVE: *William A Hulbert, Chicago businessman and president of the Chicago White Stockings, took the lead in forming the National League of Professional Base Ball Clubs in 1876. He served as the league's second president from 1876 to 1882.*

The Civil War turned attention away from Association play and caused gentlemen's clubs from New York to Chicago to go under, but it also spread knowledge and popularity of the game to a remarkable degree. Southerners learned the game from their prisoners, for instance, and on Christmas Day 1862 a crowd of over 40,000 Union soldiers, deemed the largest gathering at any sporting event in the nineteenth century, attended a game between teams from the 165th New York Volunteer Infantry. So many soldiers took baseball home with them after the war that Northern businessmen, already alerted to its commercial potential by a heightened return to baseball mania, began hiring employees with a preference for those with baseball experience who could staff company and local teams.

The Excelsiors, visiting cities in western and central New York in 1860, were the first team to go on tour. By the time of the Washington Nationals' famous road trip of 1867, in which they suffered their only defeat in Rockport, Illinois, many teams were paying salaries to their star players. Amateurism, so important to the Knickerbockers' gentlemanly code, was moribund if not already dead.

Largely because their local teams had suffered so badly at the hands of the touring Nationals, in 1869 business interests in Cincinnati hired Harry Wright to create the first all-professional team. Only one player of his Cincinnati Red Stockings, Charlie Gould, was a Cincinnati native. Taking on all comers from Massachusetts to California, the Red Stockings played before a total of over 200,000 spectators and demonstrated a level of skill that won them 130 games straight and an audience with President Ulysses S Grant.

Convinced by the Red Stockings' success that professional baseball was a commercial reality, 10 businessmen created the first professional league, the National Association of Professional Baseball Players, in New York on 17 March 1871. Charter members, all of whom paid a $10 fee to join, included the Philadelphia Athletics, the Boston Red Stockings, the New York Mutuals, the Washington (DC) Nationals and the Washington Olympics.

Despite baseball's continuing popularity, attendance fell steadily during each year of the league's five-year life span, partly because after the first year the Red Stockings totally dominated the league, and partly because of chaotic scheduling, with some clubs playing up to 66 more games per season than others, and weak organization which saw players jump from team to team. Above all, the National Association was riddled with drunkenness, rowdiness on the part of fans and players, game-throwing, gambling and activities of a generally unwholesome nature that created a genuine crisis in public confidence.

William Ambrose Hulbert, part-owner and president of the Chicago National Association club the White Stockings, decided to do something about it. Joining forces with Boston pitching ace Al Spalding, the dynamic Chicago businessman concluded that it would be less trouble to begin anew with a new professional league than it would be to try to patch up and strengthen the National Association. Dissolving the National Association would also protect him from actions by its members which could prevent him from using Spalding, the rest of Boston's famous 'big Four' infield, and Adrian 'Cap' Anson of Philadelphia, stars he had enticed to his Chicago club in violation of Association regulations.

Hulbert and Spalding drafted a player contract and a league constitution which has been the foundation of the National League and of professional sport in general in this country for over a century. To make baseball respectable and ensure its integrity, their code forbade gambling and the sale of alcohol in ballparks and obligated each team, which had to represent a city of at least 70,000, to play a complete schedule of 70 games, five at home and five away against each opponent. Admission was set at 50 cents (not an inconsiderable sum at the time), reduced to 10 cents after the third inning. Each club had to pay $100 annual dues and provide adequate police and security. The team which won the most games would be awarded a pennant costing not less than $100.

Significantly, the new league was to be called the 'National League of Professional Base Ball *Clubs*' not '*Players*.' To ensure the stable, profitable and disciplined operation of his league, Hulbert removed all control from the players and placed it in the hands of the owners, specifically through establishing the players' reserve clause (finally approved in 1879), which guaranteed a club unconditional option on a player's services and put an end to team-jumping and the chaos it induced.

Hulbert gained approval for his plan from executives of the St Louis, Cincinnati and Louisville clubs at a covert meeting in Louisville in January 1876. At another dramatic meeting, in New York City on 2 February 1876, executives of the Boston, Hartford, Philadelphia and New York clubs also agreed to the formation of a new baseball league, and the National League, with Morgan P Bulkeley of Hartford as president, was born.

Boston defeated Philadelphia 6-5 at Philadelphia in the league's first game, on 22 April 1876, and Chicago took the first pennant. George Washington Bradley of St Louis recorded the National League's first no-hitter on 15 July 1876, blanking Hartford 2-0. Attendance was not great that first season but overall decorum was improved, and Hulbert, who had replaced Bulkeley as league president in December, gained respect for his organization when, as his first official act, he expelled Philadelphia and New York for refusing to complete their schedules. Toward the end of the second season, he further enhanced the integrity of the game when he expelled four Louisville players who confessed to throwing games for New York gamblers.

The new league had its ups and downs – the 1878 season began with only two of the original charter member clubs – and teams from as many as 23 cities would come and go until 1900, when National League clubs finally settled into the eight franchises that would remain stable for 53 years. But by the mid-1880s, due largely to Hulbert's strong-willed actions, National League clubs were making money, and professional baseball was a real business.

ABOVE: *Morgan Bulkeley was president of the Hartford Dark Blues and became the first president of the National League in 1876. Bulkeley went on to become governor of Connecticut, and later a state senator.*

BOTTOM: *The Boston Red Stockings team of 1874, with famed pitcher Al Spalding holding the ball. The Cincinnati Red Stockings had shifted to Boston in 1871, and for the next few years the Boston team dominated the game, thanks to Spalding's pitching and the play of such stalwarts as Harry Wright, George Wright, Cal McVey, Roscoe Barnes, Jim White, and Jim O'Rourke. Although some maintained jobs as 'fronts,' most were paid pros.*

RIGHT: *The Chicago White Stockings of 1885, winner of four league championships up to that year (1880, 1881, 1882 and 1885). Manager and first baseman was Adrian 'Cap' Anson (back row, third from left). Among other notable players on this team were W A Sunday (front row, far right), better known as Billy Sunday, the evangelist; and Mike Kelly (back row, second from right), the daring baserunner who inspired the song, 'Slide, Kelly, Slide!'*

BOTTOM: *This statue, at the National Baseball Hall of Fame in Cooperstown, New York, depicts the subject of the immortal poem 'Casey at the Bat,' by Ernest Thayer. Published in 1888, it has inspired many to regard the fictional Casey as a real person.*

Several factors contributed to organized baseball's success. Primary among them was the emergence during the 1880s of the baseball star as public hero. A creation as much of a new species of American journalist, the baseball sportswriter, as of competition between National League clubs, the baseball hero could be counted upon to lure urban dwellers to the ballparks, where he could be cheered on against the new black-suited public villain, the umpire, who had received institutionalized salaried status in 1883. But important as they were in turning a boys' game into a million-dollar industry during the expansive 1880s, baseball writers and baseball heroes were not the only forces promoting this game which so captured the public imagination. Baseball seemed to be in the air. 'The Baseball Quadrille,' for instance, was one of several popular songs concerning baseball to surface as early as the 1850s; 'Casey at the Bat,' almost as popular now as it was then, was first published in 1888. The oldest promotion in baseball, Ladies' Day, was an established National League practice in 1889. Baseball stories began appearing in dime novels, the most popular form of reading material of the day, in 1885. The year 1886 saw the first baseball cards, intended for adults, issued by Old Judge Cigarettes. Baseball players were enthusiastically endorsing commercial products by the turn of the century.

During the 1880s rule changes also made the game more exciting. In 1883 pitchers were permitted to throw overhand, a change which some claim marks the birth of the modern game, although baseball cannot be considered to have reached full technological maturity until the distance from pitcher to batter, after much experimentation, was finally fixed at 60 feet, 6 inches, in 1893; in the same year catchers began catching directly behind the plate instead of taking the ball on the bounce. Other changes designed to speed up the game and balance offense

LEFT: *The Detroit Wolverines in 1882, the year they came in sixth in the National League. In 1887 they took first place.*

BELOW LEFT: *The catcher's mask on the left, known as the 'bird cage,' is the model made by Frederick Thayer when he applied to the US government for a patent in 1878. He made his first such mask in 1876 while he was a student at Harvard, and it was worn by a Harvard catcher, James Tyng, in 1877. On the right is a catcher's mask from the 1950s, made of heavily padded leather and lightweight plastic.*

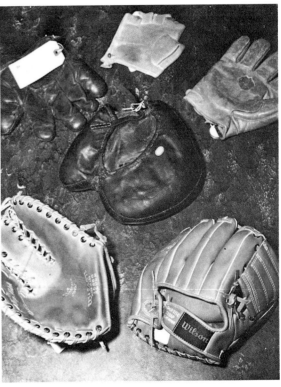

and defense included abolishing the batter's right to call for a high or low pitch (1887). Also in 1887 a batter hit by a pitch was entitled to take first base and a strikeout was called on four strikes; this latter rule would last only one season before it moved back to three strikes in 1888, the rule which had been in effect since 1879. In 1889 a batter was awarded first base after four balls. Substitution was made easier in 1891. Foul tips became strikes in 1895.

Much color was added to the game in 1881 when the National League decided that different clubs must wear different-colored stockings. The Knick-erbockers had adopted uniforms in 1849, and the first pros, the Cincinnati Red Stockings, had initiated the practice of wearing shorter pants with long stockings. For a while players at different positions wore different-colored shirts or hats. In addition to uniforms, the use of special equipment also made the game more ritualized and compelling. The first unpadded mitts and catchers' gloves were used in 1875 and the catchers' mask was invented in the same year, but it was during the 1880s that mitts, catchers' masks and chest protectors for umpires and catchers began to make regular appearances.

ABOVE: *A selection of baseball gloves reveals how much they have changed from the early types: note the model that allowed the fingers to protrude. The addition of padding and webbing has greatly increased the safety and sureness of catching hard-hit or fast-pitched baseballs.*

RIGHT: *The Cincinnatis, champions of the American Association in 1882. The Cincinnatis had been expelled from the National League because they played on Sundays and allowed alcohol in the park, so the team helped form the American Association, one of several leagues that challenged the National League in the 1880s.*

BELOW RIGHT: *Another of the leagues that tried to oppose the National League was the National Brotherhood of Professional Players. It lasted only one season, 1890, even though many of the National League's best players went over to it. This was Boston's team in that league.*

ABOVE: *A G Mills, a Civil War hero, became the third president of the National League in 1882.*

The National League was challenged from without during the first quarter-century of its existence by the formation or attempted formation of several competing major leagues. The American Association of Base Ball Clubs was founded in 1882 around the nucleus of the Cincinnati club that had been expelled by the National League for playing games on Sunday and selling liquor in the park. Immediately dubbed the 'Beer-Ball league,' the American Association permitted Sunday games and the sale of alcohol on the grounds. With a 25-cent admission, it soon gained the edge in attendance. League war, particularly mutual player raiding, weakened both leagues until National League president Abraham G Mills, the 'Bismarck of Baseball,' engineered the National Agreement of 1883. This covenant guaranteed territorial rights, set minimum player salaries at $1000 and created an 11-player reserve list. Players who at first deemed it an honor to be valued enough to be placed on their team's reserve list soon found that this arrangement also enabled the owners to cut their salaries at will, since they could not move freely to another team. The National Agreement also created a post-season World Series between league champions which significantly enhanced the popularity of the game.

Both major leagues faced a challenge from St Louis millionaire Henry V Lucas in 1884. His Union Association repudiated the hated reserve clause and attracted many established players, but the National

League and the American Association raided his players so ruthlessly that the infant Union Association lost seven of its 12 franchises and folded after one season.

Chafing under arbitrary salary ceilings and the club owners' use of the reserve clause to keep top stars' salaries low, John Montgomery Ward, law school graduate and New York Giant star, created the National Brotherhood of Professional Base Ball Players union during the 1880s. After the owners reneged on their negotiated promise to end salary ceilings and other abuses, Ward, the players union and sympathetic investors founded the Players League in 1890. The entire Washington team and fully 80 percent of National League players jumped to the new league, leaving the National League minus most of its greatest stars.

In retaliation, the National League rescheduled its games to conflict with the Players League. This move succeeded in crippling attendance in all three existing leagues so severely that organized baseball nearly went bankrupt. The Players League did in fact go under after its only season, and the American Association lasted only one more year before it too was gobbled up by the more financially sound National League. The Senior Circuit then expanded to 12 teams for the remainder of the nineteenth century. A monopoly in an age of monopolies, the National League reverted to its objectionable practices, slashing salaries of top stars such as slugger Ed Delahanty from $2100 to $1800, and others by as much as 40 percent.

The demise of the American Association ended the popular World Series, a loss baseball could ill afford in the continuing business depression of the 1890s. From 1894-97, when first and second place teams battled for the gaudy Temple Cup, baseball continued to be a popular game, but on the whole the 1890s were not a great decade for baseball as a business. In 1898 only five of the 12 clubs showed a profit.

True to the spirit of the age, the owners, who styled themselves 'magnates,' squabbled among themselves and with players and officials; sued and countersued; and further alienated the fans with a string of accusations, abuse and slander. Baseball pioneer Al Spalding later remarked that the behavior of the owners of this era, along with gambling and drunkenness, comprised the three all-time evils faced by major league baseball. Indeed, under the aegis of New York Giant owner Andrew Freedman, a brief attempt was made to turn the National League into a trust which would pool players, profits and franchises, shifting players and franchises according to profit opportunities.

Happily for baseball, 'Freedmanism' did not succeed. Through it all, of course, the game went on. Outstanding during the first decade of National League life were the great Boston and Chicago teams. The Chicago White Stockings took six pennants by 1886, five under Adrian 'Cap' Anson, who became playing manager in 1879.

The premier player of organized baseball's first quarter-century, Anson was a gifted slugger – some of his records still stand – with a gift for showmanship that gained him a popularity greater than almost any

LEFT: *Ed Delahanty was one of the most powerful hitters in the early National League. He hit over .400 for three years, including a whopping .410 in 1899. But Delahanty was also a powerful drinker, and in 1903, trying to board a train while drunk, he fell into the Niagara River and was swept over the falls.*

player before Babe Ruth. His clowning and dramatics lured thousands to the parks, and his creative vilification of the umpire helped institutionalize the ritualized hostility that has become one of the game's enduring attractions.

After he became Chicago's playing manager, Anson's pioneering of baseball strategy exercised considerable influence on how the game was played. It also earned him five pennants in his first seven years as manager; between 1880 and 1891 his White Stockings never finished lower than fourth place. Apart from drills in signals, backing up players, and experiments with pitching rotation, platooning and the hit-and-run play, his disciplinary style included nightly bed checks and fines for beer drinking. Anson traveled south with the Chicago club to Hot Springs, Arkansas, in 1885, and is generally credited as the originator of spring training.

LEFT: *Adrian 'Cap' Anson first played with the National Association's Philadelphia Athletics from 1871 to 1875. In 1876 he joined the Chicago White Stockings and played with them until 1897; from 1879 through 1898 he also served as the team's manager. Credited with such innovations as spring training in the South and the hit-and-run play, unfortunately Anson was also instrumental in banning black players from the majors during the 1880s.*

Boston, under the management of baseball pioneer Harry Wright, took pennants in 1877 and 1878, aided by 40-win seasons from hurler Tom Bond and slugger Jim White, and took the flag again in 1883. The Providence club, which had taken the pennant in 1879, returned to lead the league in 1884, spurred on by the amazing pitching of Charles 'Old Hoss' Radbourne, who was 60-12, pitching 75 games with an impressive 1.38 ERA.

Fired by such luminaries as catcher Charles Bennett and captain Ned Hanlon, the Detroit Wolverines took the 1887 flag with an incredible .343 team batting average. The New York Giants, reinstated in the league with Philadelphia in 1883, took flags in 1888 and 1889 under the able management of the stovepipe-hatted Jim Mutrie. In 1889, the closest race in the league up to then, the Giants drew over 20,000 fans and earned a tidy $45,000 profit on their way to the pennant and a World Series victory over Brooklyn.

Baseball was booming in the 1880s, but before the decade was over events transpired that established racial discrimination as an enduring feature of organized baseball and excluded blacks from the major leagues until 1947. In the 1880s at least 20 blacks played baseball with organized white clubs, despite the 1867 National Association resolution barring these players and their teams. No written rule

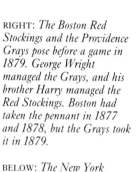

RIGHT: *The Boston Red Stockings and the Providence Grays pose before a game in 1879. George Wright managed the Grays, and his brother Harry managed the Red Stockings. Boston had taken the pennant in 1877 and 1878, but the Grays took it in 1879.*

BELOW: *The New York Giants of 1889, the year they took the National League pennant. Their manager, James 'Truthful Jeems' Mutrie, is seated center, in streetclothes. During the 1890 season, when the players walked out and formed their own league, Mutrie put together a team called 'Mutrie's Mules,' with the slogan 'We Are The People.'*

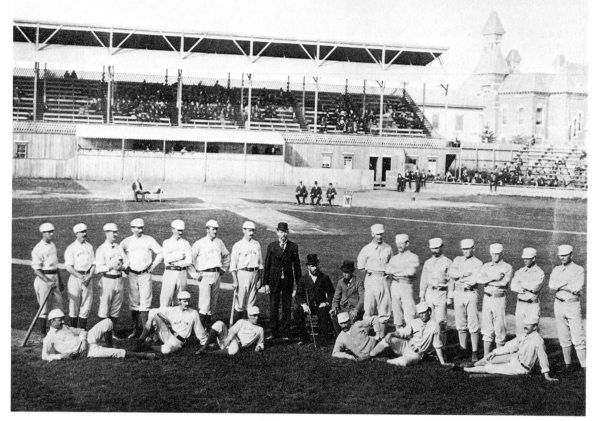

excluding blacks existed in any of the leagues which followed the National Association, but the force of the old resolution persisted through them into the National League in the form of the so-called 'gentlemen's agreement.' Nevertheless, the color line was not universally respected. Moses Fleetwood Walker and his brother William Walker, for instance, played major league ball with the American Association's Toledo club. Bud Fowler played on white organized teams as early as 1872, and the all-black Cuban Giants beat the Cincinnati Red Stockings in an exhibition game in 1886.

Many white players, chary of their jobs, believed or purported to believe that there was a law against blacks playing professional ball. Cap Anson at first refused to let his White Stockings face Toledo in 1883 when he caught sight of Fleet Walker at first base. Five years later Anson refused to play a Newark team that included George Stovey, whom many consider the greatest black pitcher of all time. When John

Montgomery Ward tried to bring Stovey up to pitch for the Giants in 1887, Anson, exercising all his tremendous influence in baseball circles, was able to prevent it at a time when it was still possible that blacks might have become permanently established in white organized baseball's structure. Unfortunately, the precedent was set otherwise, and by the end of the decade blacks found themselves formally barred from the minors and excluded from major league ball, although neither major league ever formally barred blacks.

Two outstanding teams, the Boston Beaneaters and the Baltimore Orioles, dominated 1890s play. Under manager Frank Selee, who was short on stra-

LEFT: *Moses Fleetwood Walker, a graduate of Oberlin College, played with the Toledo club in the Northwestern Association, and in 1883 went to the American Association. Walker was kept out of the majors by the unwritten rule which barred blacks.*

tegy but long on spotting talent, Boston took five pennants during this decade. A Selee find, pitcher Charles 'Kid' Nichols, logged win totals from 1890-99 of 27, 30, 35, 33, 32, 30, 30, 30, 29 and 21. Boston's Hugh Duffy hit .438 in 1894, and teammate Bobby Lowe was the first ever to hit four home runs in a nine-inning game.

Under master strategist Ned Hanlon, who picked up where Anson left off, Baltimore perfected the 'scientific' style of play that predominated in the National League over the next two decades. Helping Hanlon win pennants in 1894-96 (the Orioles placed second in 1897-98) was an amazing lineup that included six future Hall of Famers: John J McGraw, Hughey Jennings, Wilbert Robinson, Joe Kelley, Dan Brouthers, and 'Hit 'em where they ain't' Wee Willie Keeler. While advancing team strategy with their 'inside' baseball, the Orioles also set a less savory precedent for rowdiness, blistering profanity, cheating, intentional spiking and tripping of base-

ABOVE: *Another prominent black player in the 1880s was Bud Fowler, here (back row, center) with the Keokuk, Iowa team of 1885.*

LEFT: *Red Sox catcher 'Rough Bill' Carrigan (left) and Cy Young (right) frame Napoleon Lajoie of the Cleveland Indians. Both Lajoie and Young had been National League stars before jumping over to the new American League in 1901.*

OPPOSITE: *This crowd of Boston 'kranks' (or fans) are accompanying their 1897 National League champions, the Beaneaters, to Baltimore for the Temple Cup Series with the Orioles. This series, which Baltimore won 4-1, was the last for the Temple Cup.*

runners and intimidation of umpires. Widely imitated by other clubs, these unwholesome practices brought spectators to the parks and thus were generally overlooked by the baseball establishment. As Teddy Roosevelt astutely observed, 'When money comes in at the gate, sport flies out the window.'

Among those who were unhappy with the rowdyism that characterized the baseball of the day and were equally uninspired by the magnate-ridden 12-club National League monopoly were sportswriter Byron Bancroft Johnson and Charles Albert Comiskey. When they met in 1892, former player Comiskey was managing the Cincinnati Reds and Johnson was writing for the Cincinnati *Commercial Gazette*. With Comiskey's help Johnson became president of the strongest of the minors, the Western League, in 1893. Comiskey took over one of the league's franchises the following year, and the two men began earnestly upgrading the Western League to major league status.

No other challenge to the National League had ever been mounted so thoughtfully and carefully, or by men of such energy and executive ability. As league president Johnson upheld the authority of umpires, encouraged women to attend games, discouraged profanity and the sale of alcohol, and ran such a dignified operation that baseball professionals of ability, such as Connie Mack (Cornelius McGillicuddy), who purchased the Milwaukee franchise in 1894, were eager to embrace it. Johnson's rallying cry was 'Clean baseball and more 25-cent seats,' and his league made money.

In 1899 Johnson secured the backing of coal magnate Charles Somers and renamed his circuit the American League to create a more national image. He secured a Cleveland franchise when the National League pared its roster to eight clubs in 1900. And after the National League refused even to consider his forthright attempt to establish a second major league, he withdrew from the National Agreement, to which he had been party as a minor league, and announced that the American League would begin 1901 as a major league. No longer constrained to honor the National League's $2400 cap on players' salaries or its reserve clause, Johnson continued to move franchises into eastern cities while he capitalized on National League player discontent. In 1901, 111 of 182 American League players had jumped from the National League, including Napoleon Lajoie, whose salary more than doubled; Cy Young, the game's greatest pitcher; and many other great stars.

By the end of the 1902 season total American League attendance stood at 2,228,000 and total National League attendance stood at 1,684,000. The Senior Circuit decided that it would speak to Ban Johnson after all, but Johnson refused the offer of a merger. Early in 1903 the latest National Agreement finally established the American League as a major league. Territorial rights were set for the 16 franchises and agreements were reached, with significant but not major differences between the leagues, for common schedules, playing regulations, and especially player contracts, which guaranteed mutual respect through a tightened reserve rule. A National Commission composed of the presidents of both leagues and Cincinnati Reds owner August Herrmann, who was re-elected each year, was formed to oversee big league baseball.

With the establishment of the two-league structure that still defines baseball today, the fixing of the rules and dimensions of baseball in a form which has remained essentially unchanged and the playing of the first modern World Series in 1903 – all under the watchful eye of the National Commission – baseball had completed a long journey. It now faced a new century and a new era.

CHAPTER TWO

From Star Wars to Scandal

rom the time of the first modern World Series in 1903, baseball entered a period of remarkable stability and growth. Even the teams themselves reflected this stability, for while the names of some clubs would change over the next few decades, all major league franchises remained fixed until 1953, enabling the formation of the great city loyalties and rivalries of teams in a national pastime which in time came to mean more to most Americans than the clashes of political parties or nations. A great epoch of peace and prosperity which was to produce some of the game's greatest stars, most legendary figures and unforgettable moments began as both major leagues played constant schedules under practical rules. The Modern Era had begun.

During the final two decades of dead-ball play, before the introduction of the lively ball in 1920 permanently altered offensive and defensive strategy, the most important single factor in deciding games and championships was pitching. A list of the great hurlers of the day still boggles the mind: Cy Young, Christy Mathewson, Jack Chesbro, Joe McGinnity, Eddie Plank, Ed Walsh, Addie Joss, Smokey Joe

OPPOSITE: 'Laughing Larry' Doyle played second base on John McGraw's New York Giants team for most of his 14 years in the majors. He best expressed the feeling shared by many of the outstanding players of the day, who did not consider their careers complete until they had played for the great McGraw, when he exclaimed, 'Oh, it's great to be young and a Giant!'

RIGHT: Red Sox fans in the overflow crowd at the Old Huntington Avenue Grounds, Boston, during the deciding game of the 1903 World Series. This was the first of the modern World Series classics. Boston clinched the Series over the Pirates in this game on 13 October 1903.

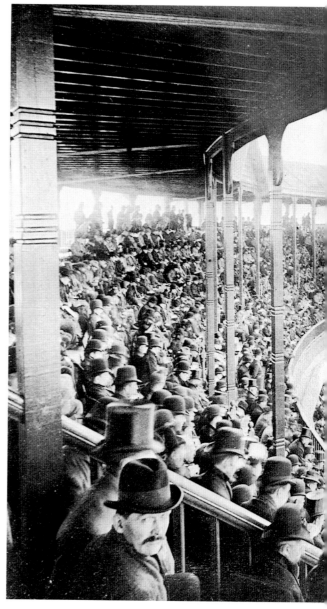

Wood, Mordecai Brown, Rube Waddell, Walter Johnson, Grover Cleveland Alexander. In 1904 the eccentric Waddell struck out 343 men, and until 1909, when cork was added to the baseball's rubber center, foreshadowing the changes to come in 1920, hitting became all but a lost art.

This era also stands out as a time of ballpark building. Previously parks had been as rickety and moveable as the franchises themselves, mostly wooden, the backless boards most spectators sat upon collapsing or catching fire with some regularity. Now ballparks came to be built of concrete and steel. The brickyard Ben Shibe and Connie Mack bought in 1909 became home for Philadelphia games until 1971. Comiskey Park, which opened in 1910, Fenway Park and Tiger Stadium, both opening in 1912, and Wrigley Field, which opened in 1914, still welcome throngs of spectators each season.

As if to prove that the game hadn't become thoroughly civilized, in 1904 Giant manager John J McGraw, nursing a long-standing feud with Ban Johnson, refused to play the American League champs, the Boston Somersets, in the World Series

on the grounds that they were minor-leaguers. Over the winter the National Commission made participation in the post-season championship mandatory, and America's most universally followed sporting event has continued without interruption ever since.

One of the effects of the roster changes during the war with the American League was a shift in the balance of power in the National League which caused dominance to pass to Pittsburgh, Chicago and New York for the next two decades. In 1904 the Giants took the first of a total of ten pennants they would take under McGraw in the next 20 years. One of the great Orioles stars of the 1890s, as a manager McGraw epitomized the autocratic managerial style in the extreme – his well-rehearsed players received orders from 'The Little Napoleon' on every pitch. Flamboyant and defiant, as a player McGraw had once incited a lynch mob to wait for an umpire after a game; as a manager, in 1917 he was fined for delivering an uppercut to the jaw of umpire Bill Byron. But despite his sometimes unruly behavior, he was universally respected, and few managers before or since have matched his impact on the game.

OPPOSITE LEFT: *Hall of Fame hurler Eddie Plank pitched for the Philadelphia Athletics for 14 years, compiling a 2.34 career ERA and a .629 win percentage.*

ABOVE LEFT: *The Boston Grand Pavilion, circa 1890, was typical of the era's wooden ballparks.*

ABOVE: *Hall of Famer Rube Waddell led the American League in strikeouts for six straight seasons.*

LEFT: *The young John J McGraw, Orioles star of the 1890s, was destined to become one of the great managers of all time.*

RIGHT: *Joe 'Iron Man'
McGinnity won more than
20 games in each of his first
eight seasons in the majors,
twice topping the 30-win
mark and leading the league
in wins five times. His 35
wins in 1904, combined with
Christy Mathewson's 33 wins
for a still unequalled twin
total of 68 wins, helped
McGraw's Giants to the first
of two consecutive pennants.*

In 1904, the first of two back-to-back Giant pennant years, McGraw's pitchers 'Iron Man' Joe McGinnity and Christy Mathewson won 35 and 33 games respectively, an unequalled twin total. Throwing in the American League, Jack Chesbro set the all-time win record of 41 games, while Cy Young, now 37 years old, led the Somersets to their league title with 26 wins and a perfect game. The incomparable Young straddled centuries and leagues, totalling 289 victories and eleven years in the National League, and 222 victories and eleven years in the American League.

Driving home the lesson that pitching was king, in the 1905 World Series all five contests were shutouts. The college-educated, well-mannered, literate Christy Mathewson, still one of the winningest of all National League pitchers, threw three of them himself in six days to lead the Giants to victory, a performance that contributed to making him the most admired player of the day. The first exemplary baseball hero, he was a model for parents to point out, and played a major role in making baseball widely accepted at a time when professional baseball was still considered unfit for women to watch. So close did he come to the ideal sportsman that most modern historians accept as true the legend that umpires consulted him on close calls in games he was pitching. He was big, blond, honest, intelligent, hard-working and successful, a 'Galahad among Neanderthals.' Mathewson served as a living legend for the journalists and writers of baseball fiction who at this time perfected the archetypal hero of baseball mythology.

The year 1905 also saw the debut of Tyrus Raymond Cobb with the American League's Detroit Tigers. After his first year, Cobb never batted under .300 for 23 seasons. He took the first of nine consecutive league batting titles (out of a lifetime total of 12) in 1907, and his lifetime batting average of .367 has still not been touched. Playing the game with tremendous intensity and consummate skill, he established himself as one of the most hated, most feared and greatest ball players of all time. Along with the National League's Honus Wagner, he brought the place-hitting, base-stealing, dead-ball style to its greatest heights.

John Peter 'Honus' Wagner of the Pittsburgh Pirates had three National League batting championships under his belt by the time Ty Cobb began to make good. No two men could have been more dissimilar; about the only thing they have in common is their continuing stature as great players in the eyes of baseball fans. Wagner was folksy and good-natured, the son of Pennsylvania coal miners of German extraction. He was such a versatile player that while he set the standard at shortstop, he also played other infield positions, outfield, and even pitched on occasion. His National League hit total stood until broken by Stan Musial, and his stolen base total of 722, still among the best in the majors, belied his big, clumsy-looking frame.

Because they played in different leagues, he and Cobb met as competitors only once, during the Pittsburgh-Detroit World Series of 1909. Pre-Series publicity for their first meeting resembled the build-up for a heavyweight boxing match. Wagner out-hit

ABOVE LEFT: *The great Ty Cobb, in his 1905 debut with the Detroit Tigers. He hit only .240 in his first year, but never again averaged under .300 for the next 23 years, twice topping .400 and leading the American League 12 times for a record .367 career average.*

ABOVE RIGHT: *Exemplary sports hero and a standout in an era of great pitchers, Christy 'Big Six' Mathewson won 30 or more games four times and still holds the record for World Series shutouts, including three in the 1905 classic.*

LEFT: *Honus Wagner at bat. Until Babe Ruth came along to cloud the issue, baseball fans debated whether Wagner or Cobb was the greatest player of all time. In 17 years at shortstop for Pittsburgh, 'The Flying Dutchman' led the National League in batting eight times.*

ABOVE: *Ty Cobb slides, one foot hooking the bag and the other keeping the baseman at bay. Famous for his flying spikes and foul temperament, Cobb literally left his mark on many an infielder of the day. Although the story that he used to file his spikes before the game is truer in spirit than in deed, his excellence on the base paths equalled his skill at the plate. When he and Honus Wagner were set to face each other for the first (and only) time, in the 1909 World Series, the pre-Series publicity resembled the buildup for a heavyweight boxing match. Cobb took honors in taunting and intimidation, but Wagner out-hit and out-stole him for the Series.*

and out-stole Cobb during the Series, but Cobb, who was famous for his flying spikes, took honors in taunting and intimidation. On one occasion, after he got on first, Cobb reputedly called down to Wagner, 'Get ready, Krauthead, I'm coming down.' 'I'll be waiting,' Wagner replied laconically, and when Cobb tried to steal Wagner tagged him with the ball so hard that he split his lip.

The year 1908 saw the publication of one of America's unofficial national anthems, 'Take Me Out to the Ball Game.' Neither lyricist Jack Norworth nor composer Albert von Tilzer had ever seen a professional baseball game, but they didn't have to – baseball was in the air. On the playing field that year catcher Roger Bresnahan brought paraphernalia to new heights with the introduction of the batting helmet and shin guards. A growing body of evidence suggests that Bresnahan did not in fact originate shin guards but borrowed their use from black players, whose understaffed teams and leagues were under greater pressure to devise strategies to prevent injury.

Future baseball immortals Walter Perry Johnson, Eddie Collins and Tristam Speaker, whose presence, with Ty Cobb, would help keep the new American League on top for years to come, had slipped quietly into the game the year before and were beginning to make their presence felt, but the big news of 1908 remains the Merkle Affair, one of baseball's most controversial moments. Blown out of proportion by the newspapers of the day, the incident serves to illustrate the power of the press to make or break careers in the days before radio or TV.

In a late September game that could have decided the National League pennant, the Chicago Cubs of 'Tinker-to-Evers-to-Chance' fame, bidding for their third consecutive pennant, met McGraw's Giants at the Polo Grounds. In the bottom of the ninth, the score tied at 1-1, the Giants had men on first and third. A single knocked in what appeared to be the winning run, but 19-year-old Fred Merkle, the

Giants' man on first, failed to touch second before returning to the clubhouse. The Cubs' Johnny Evers produced a ball and touched second, technically putting Merkle out and negating the run. With darkness falling and Giant fans, believing they had won, swarming the field, umpire Hank O'Day was forced to call the game and declare it a tie.

In the teeth of McGraw's strongest objections, National League president Harry Pulliam upheld O'Day's ruling, a playoff game was scheduled, and Mordecai 'Three Finger' Brown took the game from Christy Mathewson to hand the Cubs their third consecutive pennant. Merkle found himself hounded by the press and labelled 'Bonehead' for the rest of his competent 16-year career. McGraw's unwillingness to forgive the National League president for upholding O'Day's decision and the sensational coverage the press gave the incident undoubtedly contributed to Pulliam's suicide less than a year later.

The 1908 season also marked the zenith of the pitchers' dominance as hitting bottomed out and the National League hit an all-time league low of .238 (Brooklyn hit .213 as a team). The American League took major league honors with a .239 average. Cleveland's Addie Joss pitched the American League's second perfect game, retiring 27 men in order; and Christy Mathewson put together his greatest year ever with 37 victories and a 1.43 ERA.

Despite his withering hurling Honus Wagner still managed to take his league's batting title with a .345 average, taking it again in 1909 and driving his Pirates to 110 wins, the pennant and a seven-game Series win over Detroit in apparent celebration of Pittsburgh owner Barney Dreyfuss's new triple-decked steel ballpark, Forbes Field, capacity 25,000. Although Detroit's loss signalled that the American League had now taken only one World Series in nine years, a rising tide of talented younger players replacing such departing greats as Nap Lajoie and Cy Young signified a startling change for the young league.

In 1910 Connie Mack's Athletics took the Series from the Cubs in a five-game show of force that announced their arrival as the American League's first dynasty team. They would begin the second decade of the new century with four consecutive pennants and three world championships. In their victory over the Cubs the Mackmen, featuring their 'hundred-thousand-dollar infield,' set a Series team batting mark of .316 that stood for 50 years. In the National League, after the Cubs bowed out in 1910, McGraw started a dynasty of his own, his Giants taking pennants from 1911-13.

Although Cubs pitchers, sparked by Leonard Cole's 20-4 rookie season, led the league and captured the flag, the Cubs of 1910, essentially the same team as the successful 1906 team, will always be remembered for the infield of Joe Tinker, Johnny Evers and Frank Chance, immortalized on 10 July 1910 by sportswriter Franklin P Adams:

> These are the saddest of possible words –
> Tinker to Evers to Chance.
> Trio of Bear Cubs and fleeter than birds –
> Tinker to Evers to Chance.
> Thoughtlessly pricking our gonfalon bubble,
> Making a Giant hit into a double,
> Words that are weighty with nothing but trouble,
> Tinker to Evers to Chance.

While Tinker, Evers and Chance (with Steinfeldt at third) were excellent players, their infield was not actually the greatest of the era. More than anything else, their lasting fame is testimony to the enduring power of the pen.

LEFT: Chicago's Hall of Fame first baseman Frank Chance, also known as 'The Peerless Leader,' who served as manager from 1905 to 1914, will forever be remembered as the anchorman of the famous Tinker-to-Evers-to-Chance double play combination.

BOTTOM LEFT: A 'song slide' segment from 'Take Me Out to the Ball-Game,' written by two men who had never seen a professional baseball game and first published in 1908 by composer-publisher Albert Von Tilzer. Hand-colored slides shown in nickelodeons helped the patrons to sing along.

BELOW: Johnny Evers and Joe Tinker, the other two-thirds of the Tinker-to-Evers-to-Chance double play combination. Although all excellent players, their Hall of Fame status is ultimately a testimony to the power of the pen to make or break reputations in the days before radio and television.

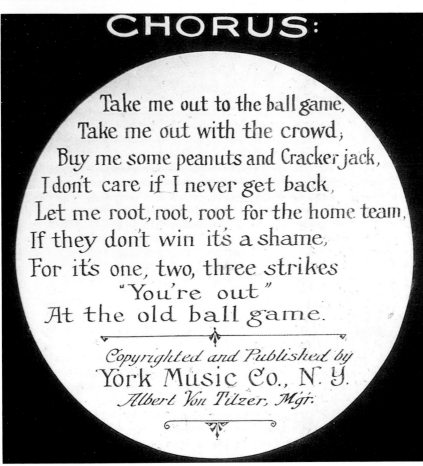

ABOVE: *President William Howard Taft tosses out the first ball at the Washington season opener in 1910. Thus began the tradition of dignitaries and celebrities, especially presidents, throwing out the first ball at season openers and other games of particular significance. The willingness of American presidents to associate themselves with baseball in this manner, especially during those years when Washington fielded a major league team, added luster to baseball's long self-proclaimed status as the national pastime.*

RIGHT: *Simply one of the greatest pitchers the game has ever seen, Walter Perry 'Big Train' Johnson pitched for the usually out-of-contention Washington Senators for 21 years, from 1907 to 1927. He won a total of 416 games, struck out 3508 players and compiled a 2.17 lifetime ERA. He still holds the record for career shutouts with 110.*

The year 1910 should also be remembered as the year that league batting averages began to climb out of the pit. Basic hitting strategy also began to change as the major leagues started to employ A J Reach's slightly livelier cork-center ball. Walter Johnson had his first great year with 25 wins and Ty Cobb took his fourth straight batting title with a .385 average. The unpopular but gifted slugger beat out Nap Lajoie for the title by one hundredth of a point despite efforts by opposing players and officials at Lajoie's last double-header to throw hits his way. And President William Howard Taft tossed out the first baseball at the Washington season opener, initiating a tradition.

Two outstanding pitchers powered the Giant dynasty of 1911-13. Christy Mathewson threw 26, 23 and 25 wins for those years (including 68 consecutive walkless innings in 1913), and Rube Marquard won 24, 26 and 23. Labelled the '$11,000 Beauty' because of his unprecedented 1908 purchase price, Marquard performed so poorly until 1911 that he was dubbed the '$11,000 Lemon.' But manager McGraw's and coach Wilbert Robinson's judgment was eventually borne out, especially in 1912, when Marquard mounted a phenomenal 19-game winning streak.

Ty Cobb's .420 batting average in 1911 followed by his .410 average in 1912 set a still unduplicated two-year record, while Cleveland's 'Shoeless Joe' Jackson, a great natural hitter whose style was studied by Cobb and Babe Ruth, hit a respectable .408 and Grover Cleveland Alexander set the rookie pitching record of 28 wins in 1911.

Frank 'Home Run' Baker got his name for his league-leading nine home runs, and added two in the World Series to help the Athletics take the championship from the Giants in the 'Half Million' Series of 1912, the most profitable to date. Frank 'Wildfire' Schulte, his performance perhaps reflecting the effects of the cork-center ball, broke the previous major league record of 16 home runs in a season with an amazing 21. His performance earned him the Chalmers Award – a Chalmers automobile – the era's equivalent of the MVP award.

Chugging along with a speed that soon earned him the epithet 'Big Train,' Walter Johnson won 32 games and threw over 300 strikeouts for the Senators in 1912, following up with a peerless 36-7 record in 1913. Twenty-two-year-old Joseph 'Smokey Joe' Wood, who won 23 for the Red Sox the year before, also made his mark in 1912, posting a 34-5 season in Fenway Park's inaugural year. Both Johnson and Wood logged 16 consecutive wins that year but Wood, whose prospects were potentially better because he played with a vastly superior team, hurt his arm early in 1913 and disappeared from the scene. Johnson, considered among the hardest throwers the game has ever seen, claimed that *nobody* ever threw harder than Smokey Joe Wood.

Underdogs the nation over never let a World Series or a pennant race go by without mentioning the 'Miracle Braves' of 1914. On 19 July 1914 the Boston Braves were in last place. By 10 August they were in second place, and after winning 60 of their last 76 games they finished 10 and a half games ahead of the Giants to become the first National League club other than New York, Chicago or Pittsburgh to take

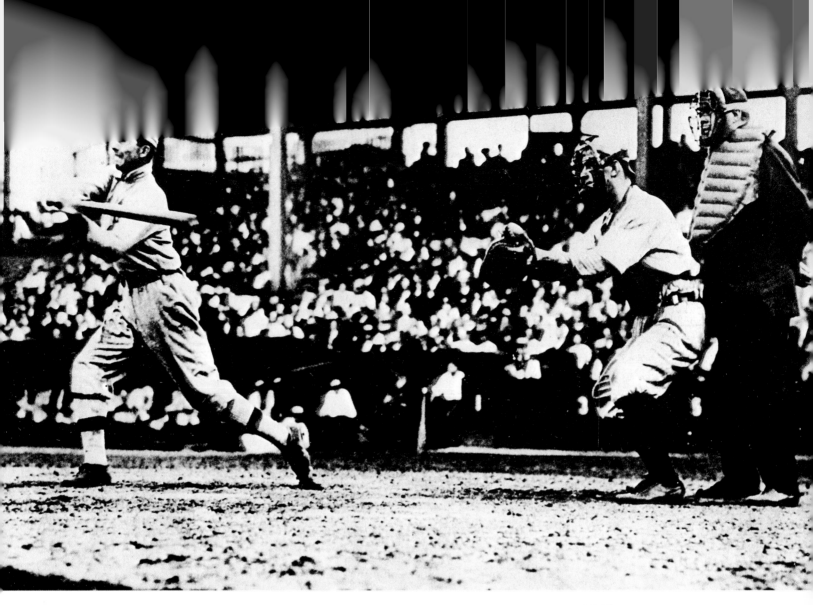

the pennant since 1900. In the Series Connie Mack's Athletics were universally expected to put a stop to the Braves' roll, but instead became the first team to drop the championship in four straight games.

Backed by the well-heeled likes of James A Gilmore, oil baron Harry Sinclair and Brooklyn's banking wizards the Ward brothers, the Federal League announced plans to become a major league in 1914. Ban Johnson, who from his powerful seat on the National Commission virtually ruled baseball, refused even to consider another major league, and in response the Federal League began raiding major league players.

The Federals landed Joe Tinker, Three Finger Brown, Chief Bender and Eddie Plank, but were unable to purchase big-name stars at their peak when both major leagues raised players' salaries. Thus prevented from making progress on the field, the Federals moved to the courts, invoking the Sherman Anti-Trust Law. All parties suffered financially before the Federal League passed from existence in 1916. Federal Judge Kenesaw Mountain Landis, who handled the case, earned the lasting appreciation of organized ball for his skillful preservation of the two-league status quo.

While the challenge the Federal League brought to major league hegemony was nowhere near as disruptive as previous league wars, its effects would reverberate for some time. Only seven major league clubs made even marginal profits in 1915. Connie

ABOVE: *Frank 'Home Run' Baker, third baseman for the Philadelphia Athletics, earned his moniker in the 1911 World Series when he smashed a two-run homer in game two and a ninth inning homer in game three to help the A's to a four-game-to-two victory over the Giants. He reached his peak and led the league with 12 home runs in 1913, not bad for the dead-ball era.*

LEFT: *Made much of in the press because of his unprecedented 1908 purchase price and subsequent slow start, Hall of Famer Richard William 'Rube' Marquard eventually vindicated manager McGraw's judgment when he hit his stride in 1911 and followed up in 1912 with a 19-game winning streak and a league-leading 26 victories.*

ABOVE: *Washington Park Stadium under construction at Federal League Grounds, Brooklyn, New York, 27 March 1914. After the strong minor league failed in its attempt to establish itself as a third major league, several of its parks saw use by minor as well as Negro League teams.*

Mack, who correctly foresaw the worst economic conditions since the 1890s and was also stung by his club's loss to the Miracle Braves, sold off most of his great stars before the 1915 season. Even as league champions his club had failed to turn in a profit in 1914. The Athletics promptly plunged to the bottom of the league for seven years, power and players passing to Boston and Chicago, who shared the next five pennants.

In his economies Mack had passed up an offer to purchase two promising young hurlers for $10,000. Picked up by Joe Lanin instead, Ernie Shore and George Herman 'Babe' Ruth became integral parts of a legendary pitching staff that powered the Red Sox to three out of four pennants from 1915 to 1918. In 1915, Babe Ruth's first full year in the majors, the 20-year-old won 18 games and batted .315. The next year he established himself as the league's leading southpaw with 23 wins and top ERA and shutout totals, and in 1917 he won 24 games and batted .325.

While teammate Gavvy Cravath set a new major league record of 24 home runs, Grover Cleveland Alexander of the Phillies threw his first of three consecutive 30-win seasons in 1915, establishing a 1.22 ERA that was a league record for 53 years. Behind these feats the Phillies took their first pennant, only to drop the Series to the Red Sox in a year distinguished by such mediocre National League hitting that Larry Doyle took the batting title with a .320 average.

McGraw's Giants finished in the cellar for the first and only time in 1915, but in 1916 the Brooklyn Dodgers, skippered by McGraw's old Orioles teammate Wilbert Robinson, became the third National League club in as many years to win their first pennant. Probably the most popular figure in Brooklyn's baseball history – the team was called the Robins in those days – 'Uncle Robbie' Robinson was known as a loveable clown, but the crowds he drew to Ebbets Field during the fourth year of its existence came to see the pitchers he developed as much as his antics. Ed Pfeffer, with 25 wins in 1916, headed a pitching staff that included Rube Marquard and Jack Coombs. Slugging was supplied by Zack Wheat, Jake Daubert and young Casey Stengel. The presence on the 1916 squad of former Giants Merkle and Meyers, in addition to Marquard, led to allegations, unsubstantiated but probably true, that the Giants helped the Robins take the pennant that year by lying down for a crucial series.

McGraw's Giants, currently under reconstruction, finished fourth despite a 26-game winning-streak in September 1916, and Grover Cleveland Alexander, with 33 wins, set a still unequalled record of 16 shutouts. The Red Sox repeated in the American League, this time taking the Series as well, 4-1 over the Robins. A young Cardinal named Rogers Hornsby batted .313 in his first full season.

The year 1917 will always be remembered as the

year Fred Toney of the Reds and Jim 'Hippo' Vaughn of the Cubs pitched the only double no-hitter in major league history. The odds against such an occurrence are greater than 250,000 to 1, but on 2 May 1917 both men, both 29 years old, gave up only two bases on balls in the first nine innings. The Reds, managed by Christy Mathewson, touched Vaughn and the Cubs for two hits and one run in the top of the tenth, but Toney maintained his no-hitter to the end, retiring the Cubs in order.

In the American League the White Sox replaced the Red Sox at the top of the heap and went on to down McGraw's Giants in the Series. McGraw, his team reconstituted with talented youngsters, had battled his way from cellar to penthouse in just two seasons; his famous arguments with officials during the Series earned him $1500 in fines. Grover Cleveland Alexander reaffirmed his claim to immortality with his third consecutive 30-win season, and the immortal Honus Wagner hung up his spikes at the age of 43 with a lifetime total of 3430 hits that stood as a record for 45 years.

While the major leagues had been battling the Federal League, a war had started in Europe. The United States joined the Allies against the Central Powers shortly before the 1917 season, but the effects of the war, for which baseball was declared a non-essential industry, were not felt until the following season, when declining attendance dictated a season shortened to end on Labor Day. By special dispensation the Red Sox were permitted to meet the Chicago Cubs for the World Series, where they managed to rack up the eighth American League win in nine years – the fourth straight American League championship.

LEFT: *The great Honus Wagner hung up his spikes in 1917 at the age of 43 after 21 seasons in the majors. His lifetime total of 3430 hits stood as a record for 45 years, and he still ranks in the all-time top ten in five offensive categories.*

BELOW LEFT: *Rogers Hornsby's .358 lifetime batting average ranks him second in career average only to Ty Cobb. He still tops the National League. Beginning in 1920 with an average of .370, 'The Rajah' led his league in batting for six consecutive seasons with averages of .397, .401, .384, .424 and .403. His 42 homers and 154 RBIs in 1922 both set new league records, and his .424 average in 1924 has yet to be equalled.*

BELOW RIGHT: *Jim 'Hippo' Vaughn earned baseball immortality when, starting for the Cubs on 2 May 1917, he and Fred Toney of the Reds pitched the only double no-hitter in major league history. Vaughn won 24 games that season and topped the 20-win mark again in 1920.*

It was during this period that the pregame singing of 'The Star Spangled Banner,' originally part of patriotic displays, became an inviolable part of major league baseball. The game carried on, but players went off to war in droves. First to enlist from the National League was Hank Gowdy, whose .545 Series average for the 1914 Miracle Braves stood for years. By the postseason 1918 Armistice the 103 National Leaguers in the service included Casey Stengel, Christy Mathewson and Grover Cleveland Alexander. Worried Giants owner Harry Hempstead had sold the franchise to Harry Stoneham in 1918; and the Phillies, fearing Grover Cleveland Alexander's conscription, sold him to the Cubs for $60,000 and two players before the 1918 season, a move that helped keep their club out of contention for some time to come.

Twenty-two-game winner Hippo Vaughn powered the Cubs in the 1918 Series, but it was the American League's leading lefty, Babe Ruth, who made all the news. Although he had started in only 19 games during the season – playing 95 games in the outfield or at first base – he had hit .300 and tied Tilly Walker for league home run honors. Ruth started

twice in the Series and won both games, compiling a record of 29 and two-thirds consecutive scoreless Series innings that would stand for 45 years.

The next season Ruth pitched even fewer games. Concerned owners had cut back their playing schedules for 1919, but with Babe Ruth knocking a record 29 homers out of the parks and postwar baseball enthusiasm booming so that attendance increased by 500,000 at Giants games, tripled in Cincinnati and quadrupled in Brooklyn, by the end of the season they agreed to lengthen the Series to a best-out-of-nine contest. The 1919 Series earned nearly 50 percent more than the previous top-grossing Series.

But all was not happy in the world of baseball. The fixing of baseball games, as old as professional baseball itself, had received a tremendous boost due to the widening gap between gate receipts and players' salaries, the extraordinary popularity of the postwar game, and the curious fact that the federal government's closing of racetracks at the outset of World War I had forced gamblers to concentrate on baseball. Giant stars Hal Chase and Heinie Zimmerman found themselves out of organized ball for trying to induce players to throw games in 1919; Lee Magee of the Cubs soon followed them, and even Ty Cobb and Tris Speaker did not escape scandal.

In the fall of 1919 the Cincinnati Reds, led by the slugging of Edd Roush, took their first pennant and earned the right to face the awesome White Sox in the expanded Series. Certainly the Reds had had a good year, but the White Sox, no strangers to pennants, were unquestionably superior. Their team was clique-ridden, however, a situation aggravated by great disparities in salaries paid to players of equal worth but different social backgrounds. Owner Comiskey, paying the lowest salaries in both leagues at a time when salaries were unconscionably low, had repeatedly snubbed reasonable requests for salary increases. Add to this volatile mix the inattention of the National Commission, the reluctance of team owners to expose wrongdoing for fear of jeopardizing ticket sales, and the irresistible lure to gamblers of a Series win by underdog Cincinnati, and the stage was set for the crowning act of a sordid trend: the fixing of the 1919 World Series by eight members of the White Sox, known ever after as the Black Sox.

Some eyebrows were raised that fall at the first game in Cincinnati when odds were placed heavily on the Reds. Incidents on the field that should have aroused suspicion tended to be overlooked, however, because most people accepted the honesty of the game with a conviction that could not admit the possibility of a fix. Christy Mathewson and seasoned sportswriter Hugh Fullerton were among those who pointed out that certain situations handled routinely even in sandlot baseball were bungled by Chicago against all expectations of professional behavior. Unfortunately, their observations were correct, but a year would pass before the rest of the country caught up. When it did, it would take a shakeup of baseball organization at its highest level and the transforming effect of Babe Ruth to wipe the slate clean.

ABOVE LEFT: *Team portrait of the 1919 Chicago White Sox. Eight members of this team, known ever since as the Black Sox, were involved in throwing the 1919 World Series. The conspirators were: Eddie Cicotte and Claude 'Lefty' Williams, third and fifth from the left in the front row; Oscar 'Happy' Felsch, Chick Gandil and George 'Buck' Weaver, fifth, sixth and seventh from the left in the middle row; and Charles 'Swede' Risberg, Fred McMullin and 'Shoeless' Joe Jackson, sixth, seventh and tenth from the left in the back row.*

LEFT: *Black Sox slugger 'Shoeless' Joe Jackson is out at second on a steal during the fixed Series. This gifted natural hitter was studied for style by both Ty Cobb and Babe Ruth.*

CHAPTER THREE
Giants in the Earth

OPPOSITE: *The great Babe Ruth at bat. During the 1920s his powerful slugging changed the way the game was played.*

RIGHT: *Black Sox teammates Joe Jackson and Happy Felsch. The scandal ended Jackson's chance to fulfill his promise.*

BELOW: *Kenesaw Mountain Landis throws out the first ball. As first commissioner, he barred the eight Black Sox from baseball for life.*

The Black Sox Scandal broke in 1920. While the events of baseball's most notorious scandal were unfolding, baseball completed the last step in the evolution of its government. The National Commission, long weakened by factionalism, was replaced by a single commissioner, Judge Kenesaw Mountain Landis, in whose hands all power in organized baseball was concentrated. Other changes in the game ensured that the American public, supposedly disillusioned by the Black Sox scandal, would flock to the ballparks in greater numbers than ever in 1920, and guaranteed that baseball, keeping pace with the Roaring Twenties, would enter an era of unprecedented prosperity.

Eight White Sox players were named as co-conspirators by boxer-gambler Abe Attell in September of 1920. Seven were regular starters: 'Shoeless' Joe Jackson, Eddie Cicotte, Charles 'Swede' Risberg, Claude 'Lefty' Williams, Chick Gandil, George 'Buck' Weaver, Oscar 'Happy' Felsch and Fred McMullin. Their trial for conspiracy, which began in June 1921, soon turned into a scandal itself as witnesses changed their stories or fled the country, grand jury records disappeared, and records of confessions also disappeared, enabling key conspirators to repudiate their admissions of guilt. The baseball establishment provided legal assistance to the accused players, and a jury, citing lack of hard evidence, voted acquittal.

Organized baseball's first commissioner, Judge Landis, however, did not propose to begin his 24-year reign with any act that might be construed as condoning player misconduct. He had been given sweeping, almost dictatorial powers by the owners, a seven-year contract of $50,000 annually, and the specific charge of cleaning up the game. Sensing a crisis in public confidence in the national pastime and fully aware of the dramatic potential of his role, the new commissioner, in his first major ruling, barred the eight Black Sox from professional baseball for life. Despite popular movements to pardon some of the players – 10,000 fans signed a petition for Buck Weaver's reinstatement – Landis refused to relent.

His somewhat ruthless severity was generally accepted at the time, however, as necessary to re-assure fans and players alike of baseball's integrity.

These events notwithstanding, baseball attendance took off in 1920 along with the booming post-war economy. American League attendance alone increased by one and a half million in 1920, setting a new major league season record of over five million. Primary among the reasons for this jump was the introduction of the lively ball. Players and owners alike had both noticed that home runs and high-scoring games drew more fans, and at a time when organized baseball was fearful of losing its following, the decision was made to make the ball livelier.

LEFT: *'Gorgeous George' Sisler in fielding action. A Hall of Fame first baseman with the St Louis Browns through 1927, Sisler led the National League in batting with a .407 average in 1920 and again in 1922, when he batted .420 with 246 hits, 134 runs and 51 stolen bases to walk away with the MVP title.*

In the National League in the years 1918-20, home run totals climbed from 138 to 261; in 1921, the total hit 460. Ring Lardner, a great American writer who also turned his hand to sportswriting, commented, '. . . the master minds that controls baseball says to themself that if it is home runs that the public wants to see, why leave us give them home runs, so they fixed up a ball that if you don't miss it entirely it will clear the fence. . . .'

The introduction of the lively ball was to change the whole style of play and strategy of baseball. Baseball owners tilted the balance further in favor of the more exciting hitting game by outlawing all trick pitches, including the spitball, the mudball and the emery ball in February 1920, although 17 major league pitchers who depended upon the spitter for their livelihood were given special dispensation to continue to use it. In the National League, this included Burleigh Grimes, the last legal spitballer, who used it until 1934. Stanley Coveleski of the Cleveland Indians was the outstanding American League practitioner.

After charismatic Cleveland shortstop Ray Chapman was killed by a ball pitched by Yankee Carl Mays on 16 August 1920, new balls were ordered to be substituted, as a safety measure, whenever the ball in play became even slightly scuffed or marred. The flight of new balls is easier to predict, hence less dangerous than dirty or altered balls, but new balls are also harder for pitchers to get stuff on. Taken in concert with the changes in the ball's composition and the new restrictions on pitches, hitters were clearly favored over pitchers for the first time since the nineteenth century, when batters could call for high or low pitches.

New York legalized Sunday baseball in 1920 and Babe Ruth opened the decade by hitting a record 54 home runs – over twice what anyone else had ever hit in a season and more than any 1920 National League team except the Phillies. Cy Williams led his league with only 15 home runs, but 1920 was to be the last year that an American League home run champion would ever hit fewer than 20 round trips. Further reflecting the effects of the juiced-up ball, George Sisler compiled a batting average of .407, while over in the National League Rogers Hornsby took the first of six consecutive league batting championships with a .370 average. It would seem modest by his later standards.

The year 1920 also marks the date that Andrew 'Rube' Foster, with the cooperation of Ban Johnson, formed the first stable black professional league. Foster's National Negro Baseball League was soon joined by the Negro Eastern League and the Negro American League. A Negro World Series began in 1924, but these were by no means the first black leagues. In 1867 a 'colored championship' had been played in Brooklyn by a league of black teams, the Philadelphia Excelsiors posting victory over the Brooklyn Uniques and the Brooklyn Monitors.

ABOVE: *The Kansas City Monarchs of 1936 pose before their bus. One of the great Negro National League clubs, in 1924 they won the first Negro World Series. Their bus and their portable lighting system were important items of equipment in a baseball lifestyle that featured endless barnstorming. Jackie Robinson played with the Monarchs before signing with the Dodgers organization.*

When the door to organized baseball was closed to black Americans through the actions of Cap Anson and others at the end of the nineteenth century, blacks continued to form their own teams and leagues. Early twentieth century black baseball was a semi-professional affair, but the quality of play cultivated on such legendary teams as the Kansas City Monarchs (Jackie Robinson's former team), the New York Lincoln Giants and the St Louis Stars was undeniably professional. Andrew Foster, nicknamed 'Rube' after the great Rube Waddell, was himself a highly regarded pitcher who was hired on the sly by John McGraw to coach young Christy Mathewson; Honus Wagner called him the smartest pitcher he had ever seen.

McGraw represented a sizable minority of baseball men who didn't care what color a man was so long as he could play. In 1901 he tried to sneak light-skinned black second baseman Charlie Grant into the Giant organization by passing him off as a Cherokee Indian, Charlie Tokahama. Unfortunately, Grant was recognized by Charlie Comiskey and others from his play in the black leagues and McGraw was forced to release him. Similar attempts to employ black players, sometimes designated 'Cubans,' met with failure until after the Second World War.

Among the early greats of black baseball was John Henry 'Pop' Lloyd, the finest black shortstop of all time and an outstanding hitter who was often called the black Honus Wagner. William J 'Judy' Johnson, who was an outstanding infielder in the black leagues from 1921 to 1938, and later managed the Homestead Grays, could have named his own price if he had been white, according to Connie Mack. James 'Cool Papa' Bell, a high .300s hitter and one of the fastest base-runners in history, played from 1922 to 1946. The great Josh Gibson caught for the Homestead Grays

from 1930 to 1946. A legendary slugger, he and charismatic pitcher Satchel Paige did for black baseball what Babe Ruth and Dizzy Dean did for white, drawing throngs of patrons to the parks.

But if black stars played as well as white stars – Dizzy Dean remembers playing a black all-star team that was so good 'we didn't think we had an even chance against them' – they never received the compensation or the recognition accorded their white counterparts. Leon Walter 'Buck' Leonard, Hall of Fame first baseman and high .300s hitter, earned $100 a month at his peak. Josh Gibson, who hit more home runs in a season than Babe Ruth, including four out of Griffith Stadium in one game, did so, as did all black league players, without the benefit of official recordkeeping. It is a testimony to the stamina of black players and fans alike that black baseball, chronically underfunded, sometimes backed by successful blacks such as Louis Armstrong, survived into and through the Depression and thrived until the diamond was reintegrated in 1947. Along the way, barnstorming teams such as the Monarchs, who carried a portable lighting system to get in an extra game after dark, pioneered many baseball innovations. Night games were commonplace in the black leagues at least a decade before they were considered by white major league ball.

In 1921 the Yankees, bolstered by player acquisitions from the Red Sox, whose owner Harry Frazee began raising money for his Broadway productions by selling off his best players to Yankee owner and brewery tycoon Jacob Ruppert in 1919, took the first of three consecutive pennants and began the first of two dynasties they would establish in the 1920s. Talent acquired from Frazee included pitcher Carl Mays, Babe Ruth (purchased for $125,000 and a $300,00 loan with Fenway Park as security), and general man-

ABOVE LEFT: *Hall of Famer Leon Walter 'Buck' Leonard played first base with excellence for the Negro National League's Homestead Grays from 1933 to 1950. Hitting in the high .300s consistently, he often led his league in homers as well.*

ABOVE: *James 'Cool Papa' Bell slides into third base. One of the fastest baserunners in history as well as a high .300s hitter, Bell was active from 1922 to 1946, playing mostly for the Homestead Grays. He began as a pitcher but moved to the outfield in order to play every day. Despite the lack of official records for the black leagues, his career earned him belated election to the Baseball Hall of Fame.*

LEFT: *One of baseball's all-time greats, Josh Gibson caught for the Homestead Grays from 1930 to 1946. More than once logging over 70 homers a year, Gibson has been called 'The Black Babe Ruth,' although many believe that Babe Ruth was the white Josh Gibson.*

ABOVE: *Team portrait of the 1921 pennant-winning Yankees club. Dominating the photo with his presence and the American League with his bat, Babe Ruth set a new home run record with 59 and slugged an awesome .846. Teammates and fellow former Red Sox Carl Mays and Waite Hoyt helped New York to the pennant with 46 wins between them.*

RIGHT: *Governor of New York Alfred E Smith (third from right) parades across the field with Yankees owner and beer baron Colonel Jacob Ruppert and wife on opening day in 1923.*

ager Edward G Barrow, whom many credit with establishing the foundation of the Yankee empire that would win 29 pennants and 20 world championships in the next 44 years. By 1923 seven of the 13 Yankee front-line players had come from Boston; the 'Dead Sox' moved to the bottom of the league for the rest of the decade.

Yankee attendance doubled in 1920 behind Babe Ruth's new home run record, and in 1921 the Big Guy did it again, setting a new home run record of 59 while slugging .846, just shy of his all-time record of .847 set in 1920. In 1921, Ruth's greatest all-round season, the Bambino blasted his club to the pennant with help from former Red Sox pitchers Carl Mays and Waite Hoyt, who won 46 games between them. By 1923, when Ruth hit his best average of .393 and set the league record for walks with 170, the Yankees were also benefitting from the skills of such former Red Sox pitchers as Joe Bush, Sam Jones and Herb Pennock.

As becomes a legend, Babe Ruth blasted a game-winning home run at the first game ever played in brand new Yankee Stadium in 1923. Built largely from the proceeds of the Great One's drawing power (with a short right field to accommodate his shots), the state-of-the-art 'House That Ruth Built,' located in baseball's richest market, memorialized Ruth's exciting style of play and ensured that the Yankees and the American League would hold the edge in profits and attendance for some time to come. Ruth's fiscal greatness also extended directly to the players, as his own dramatic salary increases precipitated across-the-board salary increases for ball players of 15 to 45 percent.

As pitchers struggled to adjust to the new ball – George Sisler hit .420 in 1922 and the Pirates led the National League with a team average of .308 – the

United States Supreme Court ruled that baseball was not subject to the Sherman Anti-Trust laws. The year before, the owners had signed a new National Agreement empowering Commissioner Landis to levy fines of up to $5000 and binding everyone in organized baseball to his decisions. The owners also waived their rights to seek justice in civil courts in baseball matters, and stated that should Landis die before his successor had been chosen, the President of the United States was to appoint a new commissioner. Landis displayed his considerable powers in 1922 by expelling Giant Phil Douglas from baseball forever for offering to throw games for the Cardinals. Two years later he expelled Giant outfielder Jimmy O'Connell and coach Cozy Dolan for attempting to influence the outcome of a game against the Phillies. O'Connell, whose real crime may have been participation in a tasteless practical joke, was the last major league player to be banished for crooked behavior during this sordid era. In Commissioner Landis baseball had found a formidable weapon to assure the public of its integrity.

Before the 1921 season Landis ordered Giant owner Charles Stoneham and manager McGraw to sell their gambling interests in Cuba or get out of baseball. McGraw, having nearly completed his current spate of team rebuilding with the acquisition of, among others, Casey Stengel from the Phillies, stayed in baseball, and in 1921 his young Giants captured the first of four flags that would make them the first team in major league history to take four consecutive pennants.

The Giant dynasty of 1921-24, McGraw's greatest teams, featured seven future Hall of Fame sluggers: Frank Frisch, Bill Terry, George Kelly, Dave Bancroft, Ross Youngs, Travis Jackson and Hack Wilson. McGraw was among those who resented the

ABOVE: *Samuel Pond 'Sad Sam' Jones moved from the Red Sox to the Yankees in 1922, hit his peak with New York in 1923 with 21 wins and moved on to St Louis in 1927. Jones pitched for six American League clubs in his 22-year major league career and accumulated 229 lifetime wins.*

LEFT: *'The House That Ruth Built,' Yankee Stadium, opened its doors to the public in 1923. Owner Ruppert was forced to build when the Giants refused to rent the Polo Grounds to the Yankees any longer. 'Ruth Field' was considered and rejected as a name for the new park, but the bleachers at the end of the short right field, where most of the Bambino's homers ended up, was soon dubbed 'Ruthville.'*

change the lively ball brought to the game, but his sluggers won these pennants. Of his pitching staff, only Art Nehf, during four pennant years, recorded a 20-win season.

In 1924 the Yankees were stopped two games short of their fourth consecutive pennant by Walter Johnson. Then 36 years old and in his eighteenth year with the Senators, Johnson was still capable of a 23-7 season and league-leading strikeouts, shutouts and ERA. The following year he helped his Senators to their second pennant ever, but it is Big Train's spectacular save of the 1924 Series versus McGraw's Giants that most fans remember as the dramatic capstone of his 416-win career.

With President and Mrs Coolidge in attendance, in the seventh game at the top of the ninth inning, 'Boy Wonder' manager Bucky Harris sent Johnson in to save the Series. Johnson had previously lost his first two Series outings, but with his famous fastball in fine form and a few lucky fielding breaks, he managed to hold the Giants until Washington catcher Muddy Ruel scored from second in the twelfth inning, giving the Senators their first world championship ever.

In 1924 Rogers Hornsby, now indisputably the 'Rajah,' set modern baseball's season batting mark with a .424 average. However, due partly to his abrasive personality, but more to the pitching prowess of Dazzy Vance in an era when batters terrorized pitchers, Hornsby was passed over for the National League's first Most Valuable Player Award. MVP Vance, who led the league in strikeouts from 1922 to 1928, led his league in wins, ERA and complete innings in 1924, and posted 262 strikeouts in a year in which no other National League pitcher recorded more than 86, with the notable exception of spitballing teammate Burleigh Grimes, who fanned 134.

Rogers Hornsby batted .403 and led the league in home runs in 1925, taking the first of his two MVP awards. In mid-season he became the Cardinal's manager, and the following year, his last as manager of the Cardinals, he skippered St Louis to its first pennant since the Browns' win in 1888. The Pittsburgh Pirates ended the Giants' dynasty in 1925, becoming the final National League club to win at least one modern pennant.

The Cardinals would win nine pennants and six world championships over the next two decades. As significant as their ascendence to major contender status was how they got there. Most credit must go to farsighted general manager Branch Rickey, one of baseball's great innovators, who came to the impoverished club in 1919. At a time when most minor league clubs were independent organizations that sold their top players to the majors, a system which gave the edge to the wealthier clubs, Rickey conceived and implemented what came to be known in the baseball world as the farm system.

Beginning what soon became standard practice for most major league clubs, in 1919 Branch Rickey acquired part interest in the Houston club. His Cardinals' farms eventually included 50 teams with over 800 players under contract, and supplied such abundant talent that after the Cardinals purchased ace pitcher Jesse Haines in 1919, 25 years passed before St Louis felt the need to purchase another established player. Long after Rickey had moved on to other clubs, the flag-winning Cardinal teams of 1943 and 1946 were still formed primarily from Cardinals' farm system players.

It was Rickey's farm products that made the difference for the Cardinals in 1926, although not without the dramatic, legendary intervention of veteran

FAR LEFT: *Ross 'Pep' Youngs, one of John McGraw's all-time favorites, compiled a .322 career average and Hall of Fame entry requirements in a career cut short by illness.*

LEFT: *Wesley Branch Rickey, 'The Mahatma,' played with the St Louis Browns and the Yankees before beginning his career in the front office.*

BELOW: *The great pitcher Grover Cleveland Alexander late in his career, battling shell shock, partial deafness, epilepsy and the bottle.*

BELOW LEFT: *George Lange Kelly, also known as 'Highpockets,' was a regular Giants infielder in 1926. He played for New York for most of his 16-year career.*

ABOVE: *Tony Lazzeri is struck out by Grover Cleveland Alexander in the seventh inning of the seventh game of the 1926 World Series with the bases loaded. Alexander then retired the Yankees in order in the eighth, retired the first two batters in the ninth and walked Babe Ruth, who was thrown out trying to steal second, for the final out, giving the Cardinals the game and the Series. Alexander, who won two other games in the Series, contributed nine regular season wins to St Louis after the Cubs released him mid-season for drinking.*

RIGHT: *Lou Gehrig in 1934. The Yankees' star first baseman and slugger who had long labored in Babe Ruth's shadow was now considered the best performer in the American League, and had already set a new record for number of consecutive games played.*

Grover Cleveland Alexander. After the 39-year-old epileptic, alcoholic Alexander was traded by the Cubs in mid-season, Alexander won nine games for the Cardinals and two games in the World Series. Then, in the seventh inning of the seventh game, with bases loaded and the Cardinals leading 3-2, Hornsby called upon his veteran pitcher to face Tony 'Push 'em Up' Lazzeri, who in his rookie year had already hit more RBIs than anyone except Babe Ruth. Allegedly hung over from celebrating his previous day's pitching victory, Alexander struck Lazzeri out, then stopped a Yankee team studded with the likes of Babe Ruth and Lou Gehrig for two more innings to win the game and save the Series.

The Yankees' 1926 pennant was the first of their second dynasty of the decade. The best Yankee team of these years, like the others a product of serious team rebuilding and the legendary management of Miller Huggins, was the 1927 edition, considered by many to be the greatest team of all time. Lou Gehrig, whose record 2130 consecutive games began on 1 June 1925, had by now established himself as one of the premier hitters in the game. The 1927 batting order, known as 'Murderers Row,' featured Ruth, Gehrig, Bob Meusel and Lazzeri, all of whom drove in over 100 runs on a team that averaged .307.

In 1927 each member of this superb team turned in such an outstanding personal performance that except for George Sisler, who led the American League in stolen bases, and Detroit's Harry Heilmann, who led the league with a .398 batting average, Yankees took top league honors in every offensive category, and often second and third place as well. Hall of Famer Earle Combs led the league in hits (Gehrig was second), Babe Ruth set a new record with 60 home runs, and Gehrig, locked in a home run battle with Ruth on a team that never fell from first place, blasted 47 round trips. Complementing New York's hitters was one of the finest pitching staffs of

ABOVE: *The diminutive Miller James Huggins, known to fans and Yankees as 'Hug' or 'The Mighty Mite,' managed the Bombers from 1918 to 1929 and won six flags and three World Series.*

TOP: *The 1927 Yankees club. Considered by many the best team ever, the 1927 edition averaged .307 at bat, took the pennant by a record 19 games, and led in all American League offensive categories but two.*

LEFT: *Lou Gehrig congratulates Babe Ruth as he reaches home plate after hitting his sixtieth home run in 151 games in 1927. Gehrig and Ruth together averaged 78 home runs a year for 11 seasons.*

the era and perhaps of all time: Waite Hoyt, Herb Pennock, Wilcy Moore, Urban Shocker, Dutch Reuther and George Pipgras.

Legend has it that the strong Pittsburgh team the Yankees met in the 1927 Series was so intimidated by watching the Yankee sluggers knock balls into the bleachers during batting practice that they never re-covered. At any rate, despite the best efforts of the Waner brothers, both of whom had hit over .350 during the regular season, and of fellow Hall of Famer Pie Traynor, the Pirates lost in four straight, and the Yankees became the first American League club to win a Series without a loss.

The rebuilt Athletics had finished second in 1925, third in 1926, and second in 1927 before finishing just two and a half games behind the repeating Yankees in 1928. But beginning in 1929, the year they scored a record 10 runs in one World Series inning, they were unstoppable, topping their league by wide margins for three consecutive years. These Athletics teams featured Lefty Grove, Mickey Cochrane, Jimmie Foxx and Al Simmons, as well as .300 hitters Bing Miller and Mule Haas.

Mickey Cochrane, for whom Mickey Mantle was named and holder of the all-time career batting record for a catcher, caught the superb Athletics pitching staff headed by Robert Moses 'Lefty' Grove,

George Earnshaw and Rube Walberg. Grove, the outstanding lefthander on the last dynasty club formed exclusively from players purchased from the minors, many from Jack Dunn's Baltimore club, lost only 15 games during the Athletics' three-year reign. A fierce competitor who was known to throw his nearly invincible fastballs at his own teammates in batting practice, Grove hit his peak in 1931, when he was 31-4 and led the league in ERA, wins, complete games, percentage and strikeouts.

An era of sorts ended at the close of the 1928 season with the retirement of American League immortals Ty Cobb and Tris Speaker. The year before, Ban Johnson, last of the autocratic league presidents, as well as pitching great Walter Johnson, had also given way to younger men, leaving no room for doubt that the deadball era, already moribund since 1920, was really dead. As if to drive home the lesson that the era of the long ball and the power hitter had truly arrived, Babe Ruth and Lou Gehrig turned in outstanding 1928 World Series performances, Ruth batting a still unequalled .625 Series average while launching three homers in a single game for the second time, and Gehrig hitting .545 and four homers, driving in nine runs and scoring five.

Under the able stewardship of master manager Joe McCarthy, in 1929 the Cubs won their first pennant since 1918. For most of the next decade in the Senior Circuit, dominance would be shared by the Cubs, the Cardinals and the Giants. Helping the Cubs to the top in 1929 was Rogers Hornsby, newly purchased from Boston for $200,000 and batting .380. The Cubs' outfield of Kiki Cuyler, Hack Wilson and Riggs Stephenson averaged over .355. Wilson, an enormously popular player since he came up to the Giants in 1923, led the league in home runs four times between 1926-30. He contributed 39 in 1929, although that year's homer title went to slugger Chuck Klein, who set a new league high of 43 on a Phillies team that batted .309 overall.

ABOVE LEFT: *Hall of Fame manager Joseph Vincent 'Marse Joe' McCarthy managed the Chicago Cubs from 1926 to 1930 and took them into the Series against the Athletics in 1929.*

ABOVE: *Rogers Hornsby scores the first run for the Cubs in the second game of the 1929 World Series, the Cubs' first Series appearance since 1918. One of the greatest hitters and most tactless men ever to play baseball, Hornsby was frequently traded despite his skill with the bat. He played for the Cubs from 1929 to 1932 and also managed the club from the end of 1930 until 1933.*

LEFT: *Lewis Robert 'Hack' Wilson, shown here at the Cubs' training camp, hit 56 home runs in 1930 – still the National League record – and 190 RBIs – still the major league record. In 1931 the popular, hard-drinking slugger, uncomfortable under Rogers Hornsby's management, hit only 13 homers and 61 RBIs. Three years later he was out of the game with a .307 lifetime average and four National League home run titles to his credit.*

The National League led the way in slugging as more and more life was pumped into the ball. In 1930 hard-drinking Hack Wilson blasted the National League home run record of 56 and the major league record of 190 RBIs. The National League as a whole batted .303 to the American League's .288, the Giants leading the pack with a hefty .319 average. By comparison, in 1968 only six National Leaguers batted .300 or better.

Bill Terry, playing first base for the Giants, became the National League's last .400 hitter in 1930, hitting .401 while tying Philadelphia's Lefty O'Doul's National League season record of 254 hits. Pitchers fared poorly in this murderous season. Grover Cleveland Alexander escaped the carnage by retiring in 1929, and Dazzy Vance was the only National League pitcher who gave up less than three runs per game, Philadelphia hurlers averaging nearly seven. Despite record-breaking gate receipts in both leagues in this year of economic crisis – National League attendance increased by half a million – the owners sensed that things were getting out of hand and actually deadened the ball for 1931, and batting averages fell correspondingly.

Although 1930 was the most prosperous season baseball had ever seen, as the Depression deepened baseball began to feel the pinch. Total receipts of $17 million in 1929 sank steadily to $10.8 million in 1933 before climbing slowly to $21.5 million in 1939. Connie Mack, owner of the Athletics, sustained serious losses in the 1929 stock market crash, and his club, while repeating in 1931 with a lineup rivalled only by the Yankees, saw attendance decline from 830,000 in 1929 to 300,000 in 1933, mirroring an overall decline in American League attendance of 40 percent during this same period. Once again Mack was forced to sell his stars to make ends meet, leaving only Jimmie Foxx by 1936 (he soon went to the Red Sox) and causing a shift in the balance of power that helped put the Yankees back on top in 1932.

The Yankee champions of 1932, skippered for the second year by legendary manager Joe McCarthy, included an aging Babe Ruth and Gehrig in his prime, as well as other Huggins regulars, but it was the rejuvenated pitching staff of Vernon 'Lefty' Gomez, Red Ruffing and Johnny Allen that made all the difference. Ruth, now 37 years old, managed 41 homers in 1932, but Jimmie 'The Beast' Foxx, in an incredible MVP year, took the title with 58.

The Yankees demolished the Cubs in four games in the Series, Lou Gehrig turning in his greatest single Series performance ever. It was sweet revenge for McCarthy, who had been fired by the Cubs in 1930, but 1932 will always be remembered for Babe Ruth's alleged 'called shot.' In the fifth inning in the third game of the Babe's last World Series, the Big Guy supposedly pointed to where he then hit a tie-breaking home run. Conflicting stories and the Babe's refusal to claim he had predicted the blast notwithstanding, the incident has become an indelible part of baseball legend.

After the Series the Yanks finished second in the American League for three years, but the purchase of the International League's Newark team by far-sighted general manager George M Weiss initiated a

ABOVE: *James Emory 'Jimmie' Foxx, called 'Double X' for his recreational proclivities and 'The Beast' for his imposing physical strength, was one of the great sluggers of all time. He led the American League in homers four times with a high of 58 in 1932 while playing for the A's, and totalled 534 lifetime round trips.*

TOP RIGHT: *William Harold 'Memphis Bill' Terry played his entire major league career with the New York Giants from 1923 to 1936, compiling a respectable .341 lifetime batting average. The last National Leaguer to hit .400 (1930), he managed the Giants from 1932 to 1941.*

RIGHT: *A major league catcher for 11 years and a manager for 53 years (1894-1950), Cornelius McGillicuddy, better known as Connie Mack or 'The Tall Tactitian,' occupies a unique niche in baseball history. Mack managed the Philadelphia Athletics, often called the 'Mack Men,' for 50 years.*

LEFT: *A painting by Robert Thom of Babe Ruth's 'called shot.' Commissioned by Chevrolet, the painting was presented at the 1976 All-Star game to baseball Commissioner Bowie Kuhn, who donated it to the Hall of Fame. Ruth allegedly predicted his home run in his last Series performance, on 1 October 1932, although modern scholarship has called into question whether the most famous moment in American sports history ever actually occurred. As legend has it, the Bambino supposedly pointed to a spot in the bleachers where he then hit a home run. Babe Ruth himself, perhaps unwilling to tarnish his image in the twilight of his career, never confirmed or denied that he called the shot; and if he did, neither pitcher Charley Root, Ruth's manager Joe McCarthy, nor Damon Runyon saw him do it. Runyon didn't mention it in his front page story which appeared the next day; in fact, no newspaper accounts of the game mentioned a called homer until at least three days later.*

farm system that ensured Yankee excellence for some time to come.

The strong Cardinal club that topped the National League in 1930 repeated in 1931, sparked by farm product John Leonard 'Pepper' Martin, soon to become a charter member of the Cardinals' 'Gashouse Gang,' the most colorful National League club since the Orioles of the 1890s. In the 1931 Series Martin so captured public imagination that his appearance was greeted with tumultuous applause while President Hoover, held responsible for the nation's economic woes, was greeted with boos.

Martin, the unkempt 'Wild Horse of the Osage,' responded with a .500 Series average and stole five bases. He told A's catcher Mickey Cochrane each time that he would steal if he reached first. In 1932 slugger Joe 'Ducky' Medwick and pitcher Jerome

'Dizzy' Dean also became Cardinal regulars. They were joined in 1933 by brilliant shortstop Leo Durocher; and by the Redbirds' next pennant, in 1934, which they took under the management of Frank Frisch, the Gashouse Gang was in full bloom.

Dizzy Dean, the undisputed king of these irrepressible characters, amazed and delighted the American public throughout the Depression with his homespun Arkansas personality, fractured English, and outlandish prognostications. On his way to becoming the biggest draw in baseball since Babe Ruth, in 1934 Dean became the first National League pitcher since Grover Cleveland Alexander to win 30 games, combining with younger brother Paul – 'Daffy' – for 49 wins during the regular season (he had predicted they would win 45 together). After a doubleheader in which Dizzy pitched a three-hitter

ABOVE: *Johnny Leonard
Roosevelt 'Pepper' Martin
bellyflops into base with a
style that delighted crowds of
the Depression era. 'The Wild
Hoss of the Osage' played for
the Cardinals from 1928 to
1944, with three years out for
World War II, and was a
charter member of the zany
Gashouse Gang.*

RIGHT: *Gashouse Gang
antics featuring Pepper
Martin, Yoyo, the Cardinals'
mascot, and Ripper Collins.
Such pregame fishing trips
were not uncommon during
the early 1930s.*

RIGHT: *A great pitcher and a great comedian, Gashouse Gang leader Jay Hanna 'Dizzy' Dean threw smoke for the Cardinals from 1930 to 1937. One of the outstanding draws of the Depression, in his greatest season (1934) Dean became the first National Leaguer since 1917 to win 30 games, leading the league in strikeouts, complete games and shutouts as well.*

and Paul pitched a shutout, Dizzy remarked, 'If I'd known Paul was going to do that, I'd have pitched a no-hitter too.' The Deans won two games each in their championship victory over a Tigers club which now featured long-ball legend Hank Greenberg. Dizzy shut out the Tigers in the seventh and deciding game after telling Detroit manager Eldon Auker that his starting pitcher 'won't do.' In the same game Commissioner Landis removed Joe Medwick as a safety precaution after the great slugger incurred Detroit's displeasure by sliding roughly into third baseman Marv Owen. Enraged Detroit fans presented such a threat to Medwick that he had to eat his victory dinner in his hotel room protected by two plainclothesmen.

A Giant club now skippered by playing manager Bill Terry, whom McGraw had designated in a surprise move upon his retirement the year before, took the 1933 pennant with ease, spirited largely by the pitching of Carl Hubbell in the first of his five consecutive 20-win seasons. Hubbell's confounding screwball and remarkable control soon earned him the name 'Meal Ticket.' In his finest game, on 2 July 1933, Hubbell shut out the Cardinals 1-0 in 18 innings. He pitched 46 consecutive scoreless innings and 10 shutout games in 1933. In the 1934 All-Star game he

BELOW: *Carl Owen Hubbell, mainstay Giants pitcher of the 1930s, was known as 'King Carl' and 'Meal Ticket' for his dependability. The screwball master averaged 23 wins for the five years from 1933 to 1937, winning 26 in 1936 and ending the season with 16 consecutive victories.*

stopped the presses by striking out in order five of the best hitters ever to bat in succession in one game: Babe Ruth, Lou Gehrig, Jimmie Foxx, Al Simmons and Joe Cronin. He managed to keep the American League scoreless for his three All-Star innings.

In the Series, the Giants faced a Washington club that had surprised everyone by finishing ahead of a Yankee squad torn by dissension. Babe Ruth, seeking management of the club, headed a clique which refused to speak to manager Joe McCarthy or to any player who did. Washington's playing manager Cronin was happy to take advantage of the situation, and fielded a team with solid pitching, Washington's best infield ever and hitting by the outfield of Heinie Manush, Goose Goslin and Fred Schulte. Despite Washington's best efforts, however, the Giants took the Series in five with a healthy assist from Mel Ott, who belted two home runs and averaged .389. The following season the Giants would just fail to take the pennant again after they were thwarted in the final two games of the season by the non-contending Dodgers, of whom Terry had remarked early in the season, 'Brooklyn? Is Brooklyn still in the league?'

Detroit repeated in the American League in 1935. In the third year of his illustrious 12-year career with Detroit, 'Hammerin' Hank' Greenberg contributed a league-tying 36 homers and a league-leading 170 RBIs, while Detroit's 'Mechanical Man,' Charlie Gehringer, hit .330 and drove in 108. Over one million fans filled Navin Field in 1935, a display of loyalty unequalled during these dark years.

ABOVE: *Mel Ott played outfield and occasionally third base for the New York Giants for his entire major league career, 1926 to 1947, and managed the club from 1942 to 1948. An excellent fielder and a powerful hitter, Ott six times led the league in home runs and compiled a .304 lifetime average. He was elected to the Hall of Fame in 1951.*

RIGHT: *Charlie Gehringer is forced out at home in the first inning of the sixth game of the 1935 World Series. He held down second base for the Detroit Tigers from 1924 to 1942, ending his career with a .320 lifetime batting average and a .480 slugging average, good enough for entry into the Hall of Fame in 1949.*

Detroit faced the Cubs in the Series, each club having failed to secure the world championship in its last four attempts. The Giants had set the pace in the National League that season in a tight race with the Cardinals, but the Cubs had taken the pennant with a 21-game September streak sparked by 20-game winners Bill Lee and Lon Warneke and second baseman Billy Herman's sizzling .341 average. Despite the loss of Hank Greenberg to a broken wrist in the second game, Detroit won in four, commemorating the occasion with a famous celebration that lasted well into the next day.

In 1935, the sixtieth season of play by the National League, President Franklin Delano Roosevelt pushed a button that turned on the lights at Crosely Field for the first major league night game. Despite the success of night games in the black leagues and in the minors, the ever-conservative National League clubs had agreed to play one night game each in 1935 only at the prodding of pioneering Cincinnati general manager Larry MacPhail. Once attendance figures were analyzed, however, all conservatism vanished. Within 13 years all major league clubs with the exception of the Cubs had installed lights. The dynamic MacPhail was soon to promote another technological advance which also became indispensable to the game – the radio broadcast.

The great Babe Ruth had recorded his last .300 season in 1933, and after hitting .288 with 22 homers and 84 RBIs in 1934, he moved to the National League's Boston Braves, where he retired on 2 June 1935 after hitting three home runs, for a lifetime total of 714, out of Forbes Field on 25 May. Although he was gone from the game and frustrated in his managerial aspirations, the game he left behind was largely the one he had shaped, and the style he had created continued through the Great Depression with the slugging of Foxx, Medwick, Johnny Mize, Ott, Greenberg, and other greats yet to come.

LEFT: *Slugger Hank Greenberg connects for a home run in the season opener at Comiskey Park, 20 April 1938. 'Hammerin' Hank' played first base for Detroit for 12 years, compiling 331 homers and a .313 career batting average.*

BELOW: *The scene at Crosley Field, Cincinnati, on 24 May 1935, at the first night game ever played in the major leagues. Like many innovations, night games were at first strongly resisted and then swiftly adopted by all clubs, with the exception of the Chicago Cubs, who have yet to install lights.*

CHAPTER FOUR

Depression and War: The Game Goes On

The decade from Babe Ruth's departure from the game to the end of the Second World War ranks as one of the most unsettled in baseball. It was a time of exceptions and departures from the norm, but it was also a time of innovation and one that saw the establishment of some of baseball's most legendary careers. Baseball, the country and the world would never be the same after 1946 – TV, integration, franchise shift, air travel and expansion loomed on the horizon – but to lay the foundations baseball would have to survive a nation in economic turmoil and a world engulfed in war.

Among the powerful technological innovations of this period were the establishment of radio and night games as baseball institutions. Both owe their arrival at this time to the promotional genius of Larry MacPhail, whose many innovations also include the use of films that players could study to perfect their technique. Once MacPhail, despite initial resistance, got the clubs to turn on the lights there was no turning back, and by the end of the 1930s, when baseball revenues finally began to climb above what they had been before the Depression, night games were recognized as one of the factors that had enabled baseball to survive.

OPPOSITE: *Johnny Vander Meer, 'The Dutch Master,' has the distinction of being the only pitcher in major league baseball ever to have pitched back-to-back no-hitters. Starting for the Reds in 1938, his first full season in the majors, on 11 June he faced only 28 men in a 3-0 victory over Boston. Starting against Brooklyn four days later, he no-hit the Dodgers, 6-0. Vander Meer was 15-10 for the 1938 season.*

RIGHT: *Ebbets Field, home of the Brooklyn Dodgers, as it looked on the occasion of its first night game, which was also the occasion of Johnny Vander Meer's second consecutive no-hitter, 15 June 1938. General manager Larry MacPhail had arranged so many pre-game festivities that the game did not get under way until 9:45.*

Radio, despite the same resistance from a conservative baseball establishment, also made a significant contribution to keeping baseball alive during the Depression. The owners feared that if people could hear games for free on the radio, they would not pay to see them; but precisely the opposite would happen. Radio broadcasts of games led to increased attendance, newspaper sales and interest in baseball, not to mention increased financial benefits to the clubs themselves. In the American League, receipts from radio broadcasts grew from $11,000 in 1933 to $420,000 in 1939.

In 1934, when St Louis owner Sam Breadon banned broadcasts of home games at the height of the Gashouse Gang's fame, home attendance was 334,863. When Cardinal home games went back on the air in 1935, attendance jumped to 517,805. When Larry MacPhail came from Cincinnati to the Dodgers with announcer Red Barber in 1939, annual Brooklyn attendance averaged about half a million. Two years later, with regular broadcasts of games piquing interest, attendance reached 955,000.

In the American League in the late 1930s and early 1940s baseball belonged to the Yankees. Under manager McCarthy the Yankees finished second in 1933, 1934 and 1935, but beginning in 1936 the Yankees became the first American League club to win four consecutive pennants and the first club to win four consecutive world championships. A strong Tigers team prevented them from making it five pennants straight in 1940 – by two games – but the Yankees returned to win three more consecutive pennants and two more world championships in the years from 1941 to 1943.

Helping the Yankees clinch the 1936 pennant on the earliest date in American League history, 9 September, was a rookie named Joseph Paul DiMaggio, who contributed 206 hits, 29 home runs, and 124 RBIs. He also led American League outfielders in assists, an unusual accomplishment for a rookie. The next season he bumped his batting average from .323 to .346, hit 46 home runs and 167 RBIs. DiMaggio soon became the object of a hero worship nearly equal to Ruth's, but unlike Ruth, who was a man of the people, DiMaggio was cool and aloof, even enigmatic. Together with McCarthy, who demanded not only playing excellence but dignity from his players off the field as well, DiMaggio helped transform the Yankee image from one of Ruthian brute force to one of cool supremacy.

The Yankee club Joltin' Joe joined in 1936 featured the infield of Lou Gehrig, Tony Lazzeri, Frank Crosetti and Red Rolfe; catcher Bill Dickey; and George Selkirk and Ben Chapman in the outfield. In 1938 the team McCarthy considered the best he ever fielded included 'Old Reliable' Tommy Henrich as a replacement for Ben Chapman (who was canned partly because McCarthy disapproved of his emotional displays) and Joe Gordon, one of the first great products of the Yankee farm system, who replaced Lazzeri at second. In DiMaggio's 1939 MVP year, hard-hitting Charlie 'King Kong' Keller, up from the Yankees' Newark club, took up position in left field. Solid pitching was supplied by Red Ruffing, who had four consecutive 20-win seasons beginning in 1936, assisted by Monte Pearson and Lefty Gomez, and later by Yankee farm products Spud Chandler and Atley Donald.

OPPOSITE ABOVE LEFT: *Red Barber, one of the earliest and greatest baseball voices, helped make radio and the Dodgers a success when Larry MacPhail brought him to Brooklyn.*

OPPOSITE ABOVE RIGHT: *Larry MacPhail, the man who started it all, at the radio microphone. In Cincinnati and in Brooklyn, he pioneered the use of radio and night games in baseball, two innovations which changed the face of the game forever. He was also the first to use motion pictures to help players study and improve their game.*

OPPOSITE BELOW: *Red Rolfe scores for the Yanks in the 1939 World Series. Joe DiMaggio is on deck, waved back by the batboy.*

BELOW: *The Yankees pose in their dugout before the game, 1936 World Series.*

TOP RIGHT: *Robert William Andrew 'Rapid Robert' Feller, baseball's only true prodigy, signed on with Cleveland in 1936 at the age of 17, struck out 15 batters in his first major league appearance, and then went home to Iowa to finish high school.*

RIGHT: *Hall of Famer Charles Herbert 'Red' Ruffing pitched for the Yankees for 14 years, from 1931 to 1946. Always a solid performer, he hurled four consecutive 20-win seasons from 1936 to 1939.*

BELOW: *A general view of the crowd at the dedication of the Baseball Hall of Fame in Cooperstown, New York, on 12 June 1936. The Hall of Fame and National Baseball Library have become a shrine for fans and a mecca for scholars.*

Late in 1936 Cleveland introduced a 17-year-old pitcher named Bob Feller. The only real prodigy in baseball history, 'Rapid Robert' employed the fastball he and his semipro father had developed on the diamond they had carved out of their Iowa farm to fan 15 players in his first major league game. Less than a month later he set a new league record by striking out 17 players in a game against the Athletics. Then he went home to finish high school.

Feller won 107 games by the time he was 22; most players considered him to be in a class by himself. Although he was robbed of spectacular lifetime statistics by four years in the service, he nevertheless managed to set game and season strikeout records, and tied Cy Young in no-hitters. The Baseball Hall of Fame in Cooperstown, New York, to which Feller and DiMaggio – both exciting players, record-setters, and great draws – would one day be admitted, also made its debut in 1936.

Luke Appling, shining star on a mediocre White Sox team for most of 20 years, slugged his way into the Hall of Fame with such feats as his 1936 league-leading .388 average, the highest by a shortstop in the twentieth century. Cleveland's Hal Trosky set the American League RBI pace with 162 in 1936, a year in which five hard-hitting Junior Circuit clubs had batting averages over .290.

Sluggers seemed to sprout in the American League in the late 1930s. Bill Dickey set the league standard for a catcher with a .362 average in 1936, Tiger MVP Charlie Gehringer led with .371 in 1937, and Lou Gehrig, in his last great year, hit .351 and 37 homers. Hank Greenberg followed up his best all-round year with 58 homers in 1938, threatening Babe Ruth's record. Gehrig, of course, was forced to retire after his record 2130 consecutive games on 2 May 1939, and two years later died tragically from the effects of amytrophic lateral sclerosis at the age of 38, but Charlie Keller soon filled the gap he left in Yankee slugging. Comparative Yankee newcomers Henrich and DiMaggio – the last right-handed batter to clear .380 – continued to blast away, and in 1939 Jimmie Foxx led the league with 35 homers and a .360 average. His new Red Sox teammate Ted Williams checked in with 31 homers, a league-leading 145 RBIs and a .327 average in his rookie year.

In fact, as the 1940s got under way the American League expressed its batting supremacy by hitting almost 200 more home runs, scoring over 700 more runs and out-averaging the Senior Circuit for the season; by 1941, the American League also outdrew the National League by one million spectators. The American League would continue to dominate the National League at the plate until after the Second World War, when, invigorated by the influx of great black players, the National League would gain the edge it still enjoys today.

In the National League Mel Ott helped his Giants to pennants in 1936 and 1937 with league-leading home run totals of 33 and 31. The Cardinals' Joe Medwick set the all-time league record of 64 doubles in 1936, then turned in a triple crown MVP season in 1937 while teammate Johnny Mize, on the way to compiling a lifetime slugging average of .562, hit 25 home runs, 113 RBIs and averaged .364.

LEFT: *Luke Appling hits away. The quiet and efficient Hall of Fame shortstop played his entire 20-year career, from 1930 to 1950, with the Chicago White Sox, leading the league in batting twice and compiling a .310 lifetime batting average. His 2218 games and 1424 double plays are second only to Luis Aparicio's as a record for a shortstop.*

BOTTOM: *Lou Gehrig is overcome with emotion at Yankee Stadium on Lou Gehrig Appreciation Day, 4 July 1939. An estimated 75,000 fans gathered to honor the great Yankee batsman, who was forced to take himself out of the lineup on 2 May after a record 2130 consecutive games. Less than two years later, the popular player died from amyotrophic lateral sclerosis, a rare, incurable neuromuscular disease.*

On the pitching front Carl Hubbell, no less responsible than Ott for his club's pennants, let everyone know why he was called 'Meal Ticket' in 1936. Winning 26 and losing only six, he closed out his greatest single season with 16 straight victories, accepted the MVP Award, then began the 1937 season with eight wins in a row, for a total of 24 consecutive wins. The Screw Ball King received able assistance in 1937 from big rookie southpaw Cliff Melton, who contributed 20 wins and seven saves to the Giant effort. The Giants took the first and the fourth World Series games from the Yankees, but the Yankees took the Series and remained so formidable that they lost only one more game in their next three Series appearances.

The career of colorful young Cardinal Dizzy Dean took a bad hop during the 1937 All-Star game when Cleveland slugger Earl Averill drilled a liner into the hurler's foot. Returning to action too soon with a broken toe, Dean favored the painful foot enough to alter his motion, placing an unnatural strain on his arm which eventually ruined it. Although he managed a 13-10 season and had a few more good games left in him, his career as a superstar was effectively over. Branch Rickey, ever the brilliant dealmaker, managed to unload him on the Cubs the following spring for a good price and three players.

While the Yankees continued with consistent and sometimes extraordinary excellence to show the American League how it was done, two highlights of National League play in 1938 will forever stand out in baseball history. On 11 June a 23-year-old Cincinnati southpaw with a tendency to wildness named Johnny Vander Meer threw a no-hitter against the Boston Bees. The odds against a pitcher throwing a no-hitter are approximately 500 to 1, and with only 25 no-hitters having been thrown in the league since 1901, Vander Meer's game was a solid achievement. Then on 15 June, his next start, in a game against the Dodgers that happened to be the first night game ever played in Brooklyn, Vander Meer pitched his second no-hitter, thereby establishing himself as the only pitcher ever to throw back-to-back no-hitters in the history of the game. Thus far in the history of baseball only five men have managed to throw two no-hitters in the same season.

On 28 September 1938 the Cubs, whose sore-armed Dizzy Dean had unexpectedly routed the Pirates in the first of a three-game series that would decide the pennant, were tied with Pittsburgh 5-5 in the bottom of the ninth when playing manager Gabby Hartnett, with two outs and two strikes, clouted the game-winning home run into a gathering darkness so thick that the umpires had barely agreed to let the game finish the nine innings. His 'Homer in the Gloamin'' so thoroughly demoralized the Bucs that they dropped the next game, and the Cubs met the Yankees in the Series. The Yanks swept the Cubs, making Joe McCarthy the first manager to win three consecutive world championships.

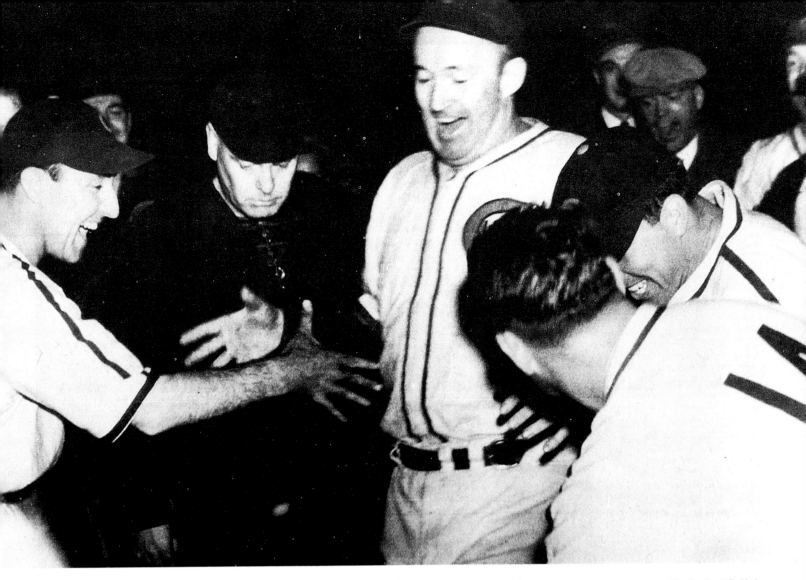

Hartnett's Homer With 2 Out in 9th Beats Pirates

CUBS HALT PIRATES FOR 9TH IN ROW, 6-5

34,465 See Chicago Supplant Losers in League Lead With a Half-Game Advantage

ROOT WINS IN RELIEF ROLE

Lazzeri's Pinch Double Helps Tie Score in Eighth—Rizzo Connects for Corsairs

By The Associated Press.

CHICAGO, Sept. 28.—In the thickening gloom, with the score tied and two out in the ninth inning today, red-faced Gabby Hartnett blasted a home run before 34,465 cheering fans to give his Cubs a dramatic 6-to-5 victory over the Pirates and a half-game lead in the furious National League pennant battle.

That is the story of one of the most sensational games ever played at Wrigley Field—a game which saw the fighting Chicagoans charge from behind to knot the score and then win on a slashing drive to the left field bleachers to oust Pittsburgh from the No. 1 position it had held since July 12.

Hartnett's smash, against Mace Brown with the count two strikes and no balls, probably saved the Cub pennant chances. Had he failed, the game would have been called because of darkness, necessitating a double bill tomorrow which would have almost insurmountably handicapped the overtaxed Cub pitching staff.

The Chicago manager, whose team was nine games out of first place a little more than a month ago, had to fight his way through a swirling, hysterical mob to touch all the bases and had trouble reaching the dugout. He called the victory and his homer "the two greatest things that ever happened to me."

Bryant Driven to Cover

A hit and two errors helped the Cubs to a run in the second and, with Clay Bryant pitching masterfully, they stayed in front until the sixth. Then the Pirates, combining Johnny Rizzo's twenty-first homer of the season with two other hits and a pair of walks, chased Bryant with a three-run blast. Jack Russell replaced him.

The Bruins came roaring right back to tie the score in their half of the inning on doubles by Hartnett and Rip Collins and a bunt which Billy Jurges beat out.

In the seventh a furiously disputed double play pulled the Cubs out of another hole. The Pirates charged Vance Page, who had replaced Russell, had committed a balk on the pitch Rizzo hit into the double killing, but succeeded only in using up time as darkness gathered.

Battling desperately, the Corsairs went back to work in the eighth. Arky Vaughan walked and Gus Suhr singled. Larry French replaced Page. Heinie Manush batted for Pep Young and singled, scoring Vaughan.

Big Bill Lee, who had finished

Times Wide World

Gabby Hartnett

yesterday's game, went in for French and was greeted by Lee Handley's single which scored Suhr. Manush was nailed at the plate when Al Todd grounded to Jurges, but after wild pitching Handley to third, Lee restored order by forcing Bob Klinger to hit into a double play.

Collins opened the Cub eighth with a single which sent Klinger to the showers, Bill Swift taking his place. Jurges walked and Tony Lazzeri, former Yankee star, slashed a pinch double to right, scoring Collins and putting Jurges on third.

Stan Hack was passed and Billy Herman singled, sending in Jurges with the tying run. However, on

the play Joe Marty, running for Lazzeri, was out at the plate. Paul Waner to Todd. Mace Brown replaced Swift and forced Frank Demaree to hit into a double play.

Charlie Root pitched for the Cubs in the ninth and held the Pirates to a single by Paul Waner. Phil Cavarretta and Carl Reynolds were easy outs before Hartnett won the battle and put his team on top for the first time since June 8. It was the Cubs' ninth straight victory and their nineteenth in their last twenty-two games.

Tomorrow, in the concluding game of a thrill-packed series, Lee will be Hartnett's pitching hope, with the jittery Pirates banking on Russ Bauers.

The box score:

PITTSBURGH (N.)						CHICAGO (N.)					
	ab	r	h	o	a		ab	r	h	o	a
L.Waner, rf	4	0	2	1	0	Hack, 3b	3	0	0	1	1
P.Waner, lf	5	0	2	3	1	Herman, 2b	5	0	3	2	6
Rizzo, lf	4	1	1	0	0	Demaree, rf	5	0	2	0	0
Vaughan, ss	3	2	1	2	5	Cavarretta	0	0	0	0	0
Suhr, 1b	5	1	2	5	0	Reynolds, rf	5	0	1	5	0
Young, 2b	2	0	0	1	1	Hartnett, c	4	2	3	4	1
aManush	1	0	1	0	0	Collins, 1b	3	3	8	5	0
Thevenow, 2b	0	0	0	1	3	Jurges, ss	3	1	1	4	1
Handley, 3b	5	0	2	2	1	Bryant, p	2	1	0	0	2
Todd, c	5	0	0	3	1	Russell, p	0	0	0	0	0
Klinger, p	4	0	0	0	2	bO'Dea	1	0	0	0	0
Swift, p	0	0	0	0	0	Page, p	0	0	0	0	0
Brown, p	0	0	0	0	0	French, p	0	0	0	0	0
						Lee, p	0	0	0	0	1
Total	43	5	10	26	15	4	cLazzeri	1	0	1	0	0
						Root, p	0	0	0	0	0
						Total	38	6	12	27	19

*Two out when winning run scored.

aBatted for Young in eighth.
bBatted for Russell in sixth.
cBatted for Lee in eighth.
dRan for Lazzeri in eighth.

Pittsburgh .... 0 0 0 0 0 3 0 2 0—5
Chicago .... 0 1 0 0 0 3 0 2 1—6

Runs batted in—Manush, Rizzo, Handley 2, Hack, Herman, Collins, Hartnett, Lazzeri. Two-base hits—L. Waner, Hartnett, Collins, Lazzeri. Home runs—Rizzo, Hartnett. Double plays—Thevenow and Suhr; Jurges, Herman and Collins; Hack, Herman and Collins; Lee, Jurges and Collins. Left on bases—Pittsburgh 7, Chicago 10. Bases on balls—Off Klinger 2, Swift 2, Bryant 5, Page 1. Struck out—By Klinger 4, Bryant 1, Page 2. Hits—Off Klinger 8 in 7 innings (none out in eighth); Swift 3 in 1-3, Brown 1 in 1 2-3; Bryant 6 in 5 2-3; Russell 1 in 0 (pitched to one batter in eighth); French 1 in 0, Root 1 in 1. Wild pitch—Lee. Passed ball—Todd. Winning pitcher—Root. Losing pitcher—Brown. Umpires—Barr, Stark, Goetz and Campbell. Time of game—2:34.

On 26 August 1939, a year that had already seen the tragic retirement of Lou Gehrig and the debut in Boston of Ted Williams, the first televised major league baseball game was broadcast from Ebbets Field, the Dodgers vs the Reds. Only a handful of sets existed to receive it and television would not be a commercial reality until after the Second World War, but when TV became popular it would, coupled with the growing ease and speed of commercial air travel, set the stage for the baseball revolutions of franchise shift and expansion.

BELOW: *An unusual behind-the-scenes photo of the man at Yankee Stadium who manually changed the scoreboard during the 1939 World Series. Here he is holding the chains that register balls and strikes.*

BELOW RIGHT: *Possibly the greatest hitter of all time, Ted Williams played for the Boston Red Sox from 1939 to 1960 with several years out for service in World War II and Korea. Shown here at batting practice, Williams led the American League in hitting six times, compiling a .344 lifetime average with a high of .406 in 1941. Leading the league in slugging nine times, in home runs four times and in RBIs four times, 'The Splendid Splinter' also hit for power, scorching his 521st homer in the final at-bat of his career.*

Demonstrating the effects of Larry MacPhail's team-building long after he was gone, a strong Cincinnati club powered by 27 wins from Bucky Walters and 25 from Paul Derringer took its first pennant since 1919 in 1939 and repeated in 1940, Walters and Derringer again both posting 20-win seasons. MVP first baseman Frank McCormick led the league in hits for the third consecutive year in 1940, and slugging was also provided by big Ernie Lombardi, who in 1938 had become the second major league catcher to win a batting title.

Cincinnati vindicated its shutout Series loss to the Yankees in 1939 by becoming in 1940 the first National League team to win a Series since 1934, taking the Detroit Tigers in seven games. The Tigers had bested the Yankees by two games and stopped the Indians, a strong contender in recent years, by one game in 1940, despite a 27-win season from Bob Feller that included his famous opening day no-hitter. The race was so close that only Floyd Giebell's unexpected shutout of Bob Feller on 27 September saved the pennant for the Tigers.

The Tiger club which prevented the Yankees from taking their fifth consecutive pennant in 1940 featured a 41-home-run year from Hank Greenberg,

plus 33 round-trippers and 134 RBIs from Rudy York. Veteran Charlie Gehringer and outfielder Barney McCosky both hit well above .300, and Louis Norman 'Bobo' Newsom was 21-5 in his finest year, seconded by 16 wins from Schoolboy Rowe.

Two outstanding batting events enlivened American League play in 1941. Beginning on 15 May Joe DiMaggio, who had led the league the previous season with a .352 average, hit safely in 56 consecutive games, passing first George Sisler's American League record of 41 and then Wee Willie Keeler's record of 44, set in 1897. Somber radio broadcasts covering the war in Europe which would soon embroil America were interrupted to assure the public that the streak was still alive. Meanwhile, 22-year-old Ted Williams became the last major leaguer to hit .400. Coming into the last day of the season batting just .400, Williams was told by Red Sox manager Cronin that he could sit out the game to preserve his average. Williams replied that either he was a .400 hitter or he wasn't, then went four for five and two for three in a doubleheader to finish the season at .406. The year 1941 was also the first of six consecutive seasons in which he led the league in walks. Never one known for false modesty, Williams maintains that DiMaggio's record is the more significant, one 'that will never be changed.'

In the National League the Cardinals would take the flag three years in a row beginning in 1942, but in 1941 the lead in the pennant race changed 27 times before a Dodgers club rebuilt by Larry MacPhail took its first pennant since 1920. MacPhail purchases on the winning club included pitcher Kirby Higbe and Whitlow Wyatt, both 20-game winners in 1941, catcher Mickey Owen, second baseman Billy Herman, first baseman Dolf Camilli, the 1941 MVP, and

LEFT: *Joe DiMaggio gets a hit in his 42nd consecutive game in 1941 on his way to an unduplicated 56 consecutive game hitting streak. Many experts, including Ted Williams, consider DiMaggio's 56-game feat to be the most impressive statistic in baseball.*

BELOW: *The 1940 Detroit Tigers pictured at Cleveland, where they clinched the American League flag. The Tigers dropped the Series to the Reds in seven games.*

ABOVE: *Tom Henrich of the Yankees takes advantage of a passed ball by Dodgers catcher Mickey Owen to race safely to first in the ninth inning of the fourth game of the 1941 Series. The Dodgers were one strike away from tying up the Series at two games apiece when Henrich took advantage of Owen's error. The Yankees won the game and the Series, their eighth in as many appearances.*

RIGHT: *Phillip Francis 'Scooter' Rizzuto debuted at shortstop with the Yankees in 1941, entered the service in 1943, and returned to play out his entire 13-year major league career with the Yanks.*

FAR RIGHT: *During World War II Bob Feller and Mort Cooper formed an All-Star battery at the Great Lakes Naval Training Center. Feller's service years undoubtedly robbed him of spectacular lifetime stats.*

outfielder Dixie Walker, known to adoring fans as the 'Peepul's Cherce.' Completing the lineup were sparkplug shortstop Pee Wee Reese and outfielder 'Pistol Pete' Reiser, one of the game's most gifted players, who at 22 years of age in his first full season became the youngest player to take the league's batting title and led in four other offensive categories as well. Joe Medwick, also acquired by MacPhail, was beaned so severely by former teammate Bob Bowman one week after his purchase that he lost the slugging magic he had displayed in St Louis. The Yankees, beginning their 1941-43 dynasty, took advantage of a ball that got by Mickey Owen on a 3-2 pitch in the ninth inning of the fourth game to gain the momentum that gave them victory over the Dodgers in the first Brooklyn-New York subway Series, their ninth world championship.

World War II became a reality for Americans in December 1941, but although Hank Greenberg was drafted on 7 May 1941 and Bob Feller joined the

Navy shortly after Pearl Harbor, most major stars remained in place through the 1942 season. By the end of 1943, however, during which the Yankees lost Joe DiMaggio, Phil Rizzuto, Red Ruffing and Buddy Hassett to the armed forces, most superstars were in uniform. By the end of 1944, 60 percent of all major leaguers, including executives such as Larry Mac-Phail and over 1000 players, had joined the war effort. Naturally, those clubs with the most extensive farm systems – the Cardinals and the Yankees – were in the best position to fill vacancies, and both the Cardinals dynasty of 1942-44 and the Yankees dynasty of 1941-43 owe a great deal to the depth of their organizations.

Although World War II disrupted major league baseball significantly, baseball at the beginning of the 1940s was healthier and more profitable than it ever had been. On the whole, the war had much more effect on individual careers for the three or four years the United States was actively involved than it ever

LEFT: *American soldiers continue the national pastime undisturbed while charges explode beyond the right field fence in Luxembourg during World War II.*

BELOW: *Bill Dickey scores in the 1943 World Series. During the 17 years in which the Hall of Famer caught for the Yankees, he saw action in eight World Series.*

did on organized baseball as a whole. As in World War I, baseball was declared a non-essential industry, but in contrast to the 'work or fight' order of 1917, President Franklin Delano Roosevelt communicated to Commissioner Landis in his famous 'green light' letter that he felt baseball was important to sustaining national morale and that it ought to 'carry on to the fullest extent consistent with the primary purpose of winning the war.' To this end players were even permitted to leave off-season wartime factory jobs to report for spring training.

Fielding a team of veterans DiMaggio, Keller, Gordon, Dickey, Ruffing and Gomez, and such newcomers as Phil Rizzuto and 21-game-winner Ernie Bonham, the Yankees repeated easily in 1942. The Dodgers, 10 and a half games up in mid-August and also expecting an easy repeat despite a prophetic warning from Larry MacPhail, fell prey to the second-place Cardinals, 22 of whom came from the St Louis farm system, as they put on the greatest stretch run in history, winning 43 of their last 51 games to edge Brooklyn by two games. The accident-prone Pete Reiser damaged the Dodgers' chances when he ran into a wall chasing a fly ball in St Louis. Brooklyn watched in dismay as the average of one of baseball's most naturally gifted players fell from .390 to .310, presaging the untimely demise of a potentially great career.

The Cardinals club that would take four pennants in five years needed no help from opposing teams' injuries. Among the greatest of National League teams, these Redbirds were supplied with pitching by 1942 MVP Mort Cooper, Johnny Beazley, Ernie White, Howie Pollett and Max Lanier. Marty Marion held down short, Mort's brother Walker Cooper covered the plate, and to the outstanding outfield of Enos Slaughter and Terry Moore was added young

Stanislaus Musial. Batting .315 in 1942, his first full season, Musial was among the most popular players of all time. Fiercely loyal Dodger fans dubbed him 'Stan the Man,' despite their distrust of anything outside of Brooklyn, and the city of St Louis erected a statue of him outside Sportsman's Park after his retirement. He was a speedy and agile base runner, and an excellent defensive and offensive player, hitting well over .300 for 16 seasons.

The Cardinals carried their end-of-season streak into the Series, dropping the first game but winning the next four to end the Yankees' string of world championships. After the 1942 season, as the war effort claimed ball players in increasing numbers, it came as no surprise that the Cardinals and the Yankees, with superior depth in their farm systems, repeated in their leagues, although in 1943 it was the Yankees who stopped the Cardinals in the Series, 4-1, thanks in part to a two-run homer from Bill Dickey. Stan Musial, whose children kept him out of the service until 1945, led in six offensive categories in 1943, taking the first of three MVP awards.

By 1944 few veteran major leaguers remained at home to play the game. For baseball to continue at all rosters had to be filled with youngsters, such as 15-year-old Cincinnati pitcher Joe Nuxhall, or with older players who returned from retirement, such as Pepper Martin and the Waner brothers. Transportation restrictions and lack of talent ended spring train-ing in the South in 1944, and in 1945 there was no All-Star game due to lack of stars.

But the fans continued to support the game. Attendance dipped significantly in 1942-43, but in 1944-45 it topped all records since 1930, giving the American League its first five-million-plus year since 1940. Part of the increased interest in the game was due to increased wartime radio broadcasting by almost all major league clubs. Despite the low standard of play in what is charitably referred to as the 'caretaking era,' the 1945 Series, which one journal-istic wag claimed he didn't believe either team could win, set a record for attendance and profit.

The Cardinals repeated in 1944 behind the third consecutive 20-win season from Mort Cooper, a .347 year from Stan the Man and an MVP performance from Marty Marion, making manager Billy South-worth the first Senior Circuit manager since McGraw to win three flags in a row. In the American League the Yankees and the Tigers, with all their great players gone, struggled for dominance all year, only to be outdone by one game on the last day of the season by the St Louis Browns. This was the first (and only) pennant for the Browns, managed by Luke Sewell, in 43 years of play.

Powered by pitchers Jack Kramer and Nelson Potter, who combined for 36 wins, and the hitting of Mike Krevich and Vern Stephens, the Browns faced the Cardinals in the stadium both teams called home,

ABOVE: *National League MVP in 1945, Phil Cavarretta played all 22 years of his major league career in Chicago: with the Cubs from 1934 to 1953, and the White Sox from 1954 to 1955. Averaging .293 lifetime, the first baseman and outfielder managed the Cubs from 1951 to 1953.*

RIGHT: *George McQuinn of the St Louis Browns scores on his fourth inning home run in the first game of the 1944 World Series against the St Louis Cardinals. The Cards lost the first game, 2-1, but took the Series in six games.*

Sportsman's Park, for the first world championship played entirely west of the Mississippi. The Browns lost in what was essentially a pitchers' duel, handing the Cards their second Series victory in three years. After the season Judge Landis, baseball's first commissioner, died at the age of 78 after 44 years of service, and was replaced the next spring by Kentucky politician Albert Benjamin 'Happy' Chandler.

Weakened by Stan Musial's induction into the Navy, the Cards finished second in 1945 to a Cubs team buoyed by a fine MVP performance from slugger Phil Cavarretta and 11 wins from hurler Hank Borowy. Purchased from the Yankees at mid-season, Borowy became the only pitcher in major league history to win 20 games while playing for two leagues in the same season.

Just as he had been among the first to go, Hank Greenberg was among the first major stars to come back to his club from the service. Returning to the Tiger lineup on 1 July 1945, he hit a home run in his first game before 47,729 welcoming fans. On the last day of the season, in a game pitched by Virgil 'Fire' Trucks, just released from the Navy, Greenberg blasted a dramatic grand-slam home run in St Louis to stop the Browns from repeating and take the pennant home to Detroit.

ABOVE: *Sportsman's Park in St Louis as it appeared during the 1944 World Series. The Browns owned the park and rented it to the Cardinals. The year 1944 marked the third straight flag and second Series win in three years for the Cardinals, and the first and only flag for the Browns since they joined the league in 1902.*

RIGHT: *Jack Roosevelt Robinson becomes the first black man in this century to sign a contract with white organized baseball, on 28 August 1945. The signing with the Montreal Royals of the International League, a Brooklyn Dodgers farm club, was witnessed in Montreal by (left to right) Branch Rickey, president of the Dodgers; Hector Racine, president of the Royals; and J Romeo Gauvreau, vice president of the Royals.*

BELOW: *Pete Gray, the one-armed outfielder, achieved considerable success playing semi-pro ball and got a chance in the majors when World War II depleted the lineups. He played 77 games for the St Louis Browns in 1945 and proved to be a great draw, but was sidelined when the regulars returned from the services.*

Pete Gray, the one-armed outfielder, played 77 games for the Browns in 1945, and proved to be a great draw. But with the loss of the pennant to the Tigers and the return of the regular players, his major league career, like that of many irregular players, came to an end. The astonishing number of fans who watched the Tigers take the Series from the Cubs in seven games in 1945 in many ways signalled the return of baseball to business as usual. The war was over. But only a handful of people knew that a revolution had also begun. During the 1945 season Branch Rickey, who had taken over as the Dodgers' general manager when MacPhail entered the service, quietly signed three black Americans to the Dodgers organization. One of them, signed on 28 August 1945 and sent to Brooklyn's Montreal farm club, was Jackie Robinson.

Almost all the prewar stars were back on the diamond in 1946, and enthusiastic fans set attendance records across the boards. Hank Greenberg hit 44 home runs and Bob Feller, completing the most games since Walter Johnson in 1910, set a new American League strikeout record. Ted Williams, with plenty of help from Dom DiMaggio, Johnny Pesky, Rudy York and Bobby Doerr, led the Red Sox to their first pennant since 1918. In the National League, Stan Musial spirited the Cardinals to the pennant with league-leading marks in seven offensive categories, but not before the Cardinals faced the Dodgers in the first pennant playoff in major league

history. The Cardinals went on to make it four pennants and three world championships in five years.

It was an exciting Series and an exciting year on the field, but in 1946 organized baseball also faced two separate but related challenges that would have precedent-setting repercussions in the way players related to the game. In the spring of 1946 Mexican millionaire Jorge Pasquel announced plans to form a third major league to compete with the two already in existence. Following time-honored practice he set about building his league by raiding the American majors for players. Stan Musial considered a handsome offer and did not accept, but the few major league players who did, mostly from the Senior Circuit, included Sal Maglie, Max Lanier and Mickey Owen. Commissioner Chandler outlawed the Mexican League and barred American players who jumped to it from playing in the States for five years.

Mickey Owen was back in the States in August and the Mexican League never got off the ground, but the Mexican government quite understandably resented Chandler's declaration of illegality and American players were furious at the blacklisting. When Danny Gardella, one of seven players who jumped from the Giants and returned to the States, took the owners to court, the executives retreated from their weak legal position, settled with Gardella and granted amnesty to jumping players, demonstrating to all who could hear that the baseball establishment was neither omniscient nor invincible.

That same spring, while major strikes took place throughout the United States, former examiner for the National Labor Relations Board attorney Robert Murphy formed the American Baseball Guild. Pirate players came very close to striking against owner Bill Benswanger, and players in both leagues were seriously united in their grievances, which centered around lack of financial security. With Murphy verging on the formation of a real players' union and the wealthy Mexicans ready to buy up dissatisfied players, Chandler agreed to hold discussions with players' delegates. That September the owners agreed to such players' benefits as a $5000 minimum salary, limits on annual salary cuts, a pension fund, and a players' allowance for spring training, known ever since as 'Murphy money.' While these concessions for the moment forestalled unionization, the confrontation reduced the players' feelings of impotence and set the stage for the revolutionary changes to come, including the formation of the powerful Major League Baseball Players' Association.

Likewise new in the postwar air was the growing awareness, shared by many thoughtful observers, that if blacks and other minorities were good enough to die for their country, they were good enough to play baseball in it. The expansive openness to social change in postwar America, coupled with technological advances awaiting commercial exploitation, paved the way for one of baseball's most exciting and precedent-setting eras.

TOP: *Enos Bradsher 'Country' Slaughter, Cardinal outfielder, slides across the plate with the winning run of the 1946 World Series in the eighth inning of the seventh game at Sportsman's Park, St Louis.*

ABOVE: *Commissioner of Baseball Albert Benjamin 'Happy' Chandler throws out the first ball at the 1947 World Series. The former Kentucky governor succeeded Commissioner Landis in Spring 1945.*

CHAPTER FIVE

Integration and Emigration: The Fabled Years

OPPOSITE: *Re-enacting a timeless baseball scenario, Dodgers manager Leo 'The Lip' Durocher and pitcher Whit Wyatt rush in to protest umpire Bill McGowan's ball four call on Joe Gordon in the 1941 Series.*

RIGHT: *Jackie Robinson, shown here in 1949, had more than proven himself in the majors. Playing 156 games at second base, in 1949 Robinson led the National League in stolen bases with 37 and in batting with a sizzling .342 average.*

ABOVE: *Branch Rickey, 'The Mahatma,' as he appeared when he brought Robinson up to play for the Dodgers. Breaking the color line is only one achievement baseball owes to this bold innovator.*

True as it is that baseball has always reflected the larger patterns of American society, at least in the case of integration major league baseball was a few steps ahead of a country that was broadening its social horizons after World War II. The effects of social change and of the rapid thrust of technological advance, which through the development of commercial air travel and television made possible the first major league franchise shifts in half a century, would influence baseball through the 1950s. But regardless of these historical processes, the epic battles on the field between the Yankees and the Dodgers and those who battled them supplied more than enough heroes and deeds to make the 1950s stand out as one of the fabled golden ages of baseball.

History has shown us that if Branch Rickey and Jackie Robinson were not the first men to attempt to break baseball's self-imposed color line, they definitely had the best timing. Like many canny baseball men, Rickey had eyed the untapped pool of black baseball talent for some time, but he wisely waited until after the death of Commissioner Landis before he quietly made the move of signing three black Americans to the Dodgers organization in 1945. He had previously circulated a story to cover scouts checking out promising black talent that the Dodgers organization was creating a black team to compete in the black leagues. Although he never had any doubt of Robinson's talent, Rickey assigned him and two other black players to Dodger minor league affiliates rather than move too quickly. It was some time after he had assured himself that Jackie Robinson had the forbearance and strength of character as well as the talent to be the first black man to play major league ball in the twentieth century that he chose his moment to make the announcement that Robinson would play major league ball in Brooklyn.

During 1947 spring training in Havana, feisty Leo

'The Lip' Durocher, who had been accused of gambling on more than one occasion, spotted his former general manager Larry MacPhail, with whom he was still feuding, consorting with two well-known gamblers in a private box. Durocher was heard to wonder aloud if there were two sets of rules in baseball, one for managers and one for owners. MacPhail, also currently embroiled in acrimonious wrangling with Durocher's current boss, Branch Rickey, was not one to take such an accusation quietly, and after further escalation of public hostilities, the affair resulted in man. Other clubs promised to follow suit. League president Ford Frick was forced to take a bold stand: 'I do not care if half the league strikes. All [who do] will be suspended and I do not care if it wrecks the National League for five years. This is the United States of America and one citizen has as much right to play as another.'

Robinson had to put up with constant verbal abuse, intentional spiking and many more subtle forms of racism that first season. Despite the pressure Robinson stole 29 bases and batted a respectable .297, turning in a Rookie of the Year performance that guaranteed him a spot on a Dodgers club that won six pennants in the next 10 years.

In 1947 the Dodgers met the Yankees in the first of six 'Subway Series' that New York and Brooklyn would play between 1947 and 1956. These epic battles between the proletariat Bums and the aristocratic Yankees galvanized a generation of baseball fans. The dramatic 1947 Series, which featured unforgettable plays from Dodger Cookie Lavagetto, who hit a ninth-inning double; Yankee Floyd Bevens, who pitched a great fourth game; and Brooklyn's Al Gionfriddo, who made an 'impossible' catch (none of them were ever to play in another major league game), went to the Yankees in seven. This was the first Series ever televised, and helped by a modest $65,000 paid for video rights, the first Series to produce total receipts of over $2 million.

Business was good. In 1947 the National League became the first league to log over 10 million paying customers. The Giants set a new team home run record with 221: Johnny Mize hit 51 himself, tying the Pirates' Ralph Kiner, who led the league with 23 in the previous season, his rookie year, for league honors. Willard Marshall hit 36 homers, Walker Cooper hit 35 and Bobby Thomson hit 29. Despite this kind of hitting, Cincinnati hurler Ewell Blackwell won 16 games in a row for a 22-win season. In the American League, Ted Williams became the first hitter in his league to take a second Triple Crown, while Yankee vets Joe DiMaggio and Tommy Henrich and young pitchers Allie Reynolds and Joe Page sparked a 19-game winning streak that helped propel the Yankees to the top.

Part way through the 1947 season Larry Doby came up to the Cleveland Indians to become the first black player in the American League, and in 1948 the legendary black pitcher Satchel Paige, at 42 years of age the major league's oldest rookie, was signed to the Indians by Bill Veeck. Veeck's purchase of Paige was assumed by some to be a publicity stunt, of which Veeck was a past master, but the veteran hero of the Negro Leagues proved to be more than a relic on display. He shut out the White Sox at Comiskey Park on 13 August, 5-0, and shut them down again 1-0 in Cleveland one week later before 78,382 fans, the largest crowd ever to attend a night game to date. Subject like all players to the encroachments of age, his career in the majors would not be extensive, but in his American League debut Paige showed little diminution of either his fabled pitching prowess or his remarkable drawing power.

Undoubtedly, Paige's 6-1 record and 2.47 ERA contributed to the Indians' first pennant since 1920,

ABOVE: *Satchel Paige, superstar pitcher in the Negro Leagues but at 42 years of age the oldest rookie in the majors, was signed to the Cleveland Indians in 1948 by Bill Veeck. Many assumed that Veeck had signed him only for the publicity, but Paige proved otherwise by shutting out the White Sox on 13 August, 5-0, and stopping the Sox again before 78,382 fans in Cleveland, 1-0. His six wins and 2.47 ERA helped the Indians to their first pennant since 1920.*

Durocher being suspended for a year by Commissioner Chandler, who seemed to harbor a particular dislike for him. The Yankees and the Dodgers received $2000 fines for impugning baseball's good name, and veteran Burt Shotton was tapped by the Dodgers to replace Durocher for the season.

At the height of the commotion, about one week before the opening of the 1947 season, Rickey announced that the Dodgers had bought Jackie Robinson's contract from Montreal. Immediately, Rickey and Robinson were put to the test. Some Dodgers asked to be traded rather than play on the same team with a black man. In fact, the tide of racial reaction, both personal and institutional, reached such proportions that the Cardinals threatened to strike rather than play against a team with a black

ABOVE: *Al Gionfriddo, Dodgers outfielder, making what many consider the greatest catch in World Series play, on 5 October 1947. His remarkable running, leaping grab of a DiMaggio smash in the sixth inning of the sixth game saved the game for Brooklyn and forced the Series into a seventh game.*

LEFT: *Johnny Mize, first baseman for the Giants from 1942 to 1949, takes a cut during a game with the Boston Braves in February 1946 Grapefruit League action. A solid hitter with a .312 lifetime batting average, Mize hit a league-leading 40 homers for the Giants in 1948.*

RIGHT: *The great Charles Dillon 'Casey' Stengel managed the Yankees from 1949 to 1960, bringing home ten pennants and seven World Series victories. He has skippered and won more Series games than any other manager.*

BELOW: *Johnny Sain, who won a league-leading 24 games for the Braves in 1948, receives congratulations from his teammates after pitching a 1-0 victory over the Cleveland Indians in the opening game of the 1948 World Series.*

but most credit for the 1948 flag must go to playing manager Lou Boudreau. Batting .355 and taking MVP honors while skippering his club, Boudreau almost singlehandedly preserved the flag for Cleveland by hitting two home runs and two singles in the Indians' 8-3 victory over the Red Sox in that year's single game playoff, the first ever in American League history.

Leo 'The Lip' Durocher returned to manage the Dodgers in 1948, but not for long. When Giants owner Horace Stoneham approached Branch Rickey in mid-season to explore hiring Burt Shotton to replace Mel Ott, Rickey, by now fed up with The Lip himself, offered Durocher to Stoneham instead. The baseball world was astounded to hear of a 16 July managerial switch between traditionally warring clubs that saw Durocher go to the Giants, Shotton recalled to the Dodgers, and likeable but unsuccessful Ott kicked upstairs in the Giants organization. Regardless, it was the Boston Braves, all but forgotten in the National League, who topped their league for their first pennant in 34 years.

Eddie Stanky's hitting was an important ingredient in the Braves' success, but it was the superb pitching of Johnny Sain (24 wins) and future Hall-of-Famer Warren Spahn that carried the day. Opposing teams soon learned to appreciate the ditty 'Spahn and Sain/Then pray for rain.' The Braves, however, suffered from lack of depth in the Series, which they eventually dropped to the Indians in six games after several dramatic turnarounds. For the Tribe, this was their first World Championship in 28 years. Also in 1948, Stan Musial turned in the best all-round season of his 22-year career, leading the league in eight categories and hitting 39 homers, just short of the league season record of 40 shared that year by Ralph Kiner and Johnny Mize.

The Yankees' third place finish in 1948 spelled the end for manager Bucky Harris. He was replaced for the 1949 season by Charles Dillon 'Casey' Stengel, former National League outfielder and manager of the Dodgers and the Braves during the 1930s, who had recently managed the Oakland Oaks of the Pacific League with considerably more success. Although his clownish ways and fractured English – soon dubbed 'Stengelese' – appeared contrary to the dignified Yankee image, he was an unusually thoughtful and farsighted manager, as evidenced in his reforms of the Yankee farm system. Given talent to work with, Stengel created a winning phenomenon that is as impressive now as it was then.

In 1949 Stengel relied on veterans Phil Rizzuto and Tommy Henrich (DiMaggio and Yogi Berra were sidelined by injuries most of the season) and added Hank Bauer, Jerry Coleman and Bobby Brown in a successful pennant bid that saw the Yankees edge the Red Sox in a final two-game series and again brought the Bronx Bombers face-to-face with their archrivals, the Brooklyn Dodgers.

Fired by the 1949 MVP year of Jackie Robinson, his best all-round season ever, the Dodgers beat out the Cardinals by winning the last game of the season in the tenth inning, a style that would become their hallmark. But the Yankees took the 1949 Series to mark the first of five consecutive World Champion-

ships and 10 pennants they would win under the phenomenal Casey Stengel. During the same decade, the Dodgers were destined to dominate their league almost as thoroughly, if for slightly different reasons.

Despite Robinson's success, most other clubs were still reluctant to sign black players. This gave the Dodgers the pick of the finest black talent; in addition, blacks coming up to the majors understandably preferred the Dodgers and the National League, where the ground had been more thoroughly broken and they could play alongside established black stars. The Giants signed their first blacks in 1949, Hank Thompson and Monte Irvin, and sent them to their Jersey City farm club; that year Roy Campanella and Don Newcombe played their first full seasons for Brooklyn. In concert with the Rickey-built club of Pee Wee Reese, Gil Hodges, Billy Cox, Carl Furillo and Duke Snider, Brooklyn's great black players supplied the key to the coming era of Dodger domination, just as black players were to give the National League the edge in hitting for some time to come.

As baseball moved into the 1950s TV began to affect profoundly the way sports were financed. No war clouds hung over the country as they had at the beginning of the 1940s, and Americans moved into the prosperous new decade with more leisure and enthusiasm and money to spend on sports than ever before. Due to TV, baseball teams that had depended on the support of their town or region now competed in a national market. At the same time that TV freed clubs from dependence on ticket sales, it spread interest in baseball. Franchises which had formerly numbered spectators in the thousands took note that in 1951 three million family TV sets were tuned to watch Bobby Thomson hit his famous World Series home run. Several million others watched in bars.

The feeling that major league clubs were no longer bound to their traditional home towns set the stage for the first franchise shifts since the beginning of the century. At the same time a new breed of owner came into the game. As baseball became big business – revenue from TV broadcasts alone would reach $27.5 million in 1966 – the 'amateur' owners of the preceding decades, men motivated primarily by their love of baseball, were gradually replaced by businessmen who looked upon baseball as they would any other business, as a profitmaking activity. One indication of this shift was the owners' refusal in 1950 to renew Commissioner Chandler's contract. They had had enough of dictatorial commissioners with long contracts. Their appointment of National League President Ford Frick to a three-year contract to commence in 1951 indicated that they wanted a commissioner with a more practical business orientation.

ABOVE LEFT: *Lou Boudreau, shortstop for the Indians from 1938 to 1950 and playing manager from 1942 to 1950, peers out of the Cleveland dugout. He also managed the Red Sox from 1952 to 1954, the Athletics from 1955 to 1957, and the Cubs in 1960.*

ABOVE: *Dodgers catcher Roy Campanella congratulates pitcher Don Newcombe on his fifteenth win of the 1955 season at Ebbets Field where he stung the Cards 12-3 on 15 July.*

ABOVE: *Giants manager Leo Durocher dances with glee as Bobby Thomson rounds the bases after clouting the 'home run heard 'round the world.' His ninth-inning homer snatched the 1951 flag from Brooklyn.*

ABOVE RIGHT: *Connie Mack (left), 86-year-old owner-manager of the Athletics, accepts a plaque from American League president William Harridge commemorating his 50 years as manager in the league.*

Another indication of the changing times was the retirement of Connie Mack, field manager of the Philadelphia Athletics for 50 seasons. Fifty years of service for any one franchise is not the sort of record that can reasonably be expected to be seen again under today's financial pressures. In related developments, TV and the siphoning off of the best black talent into the majors combined during the 1950s to do away with the thriving black leagues, and to a certain extent with black spectator participation in baseball, an alienation from the major leagues among the black public that has continued to become even more pronounced in recent years. Likewise, TV, at least for a while, limited attendance at minor league and local games. After all, through the miracle of electronics anyone could see major league baseball anywhere.

This was the era of bigness – big powers, big corporations, big sports, big profits – and it seems only fitting that two big teams, the Dodgers and the Yankees, should almost totally dominate baseball.

The team the Dodgers fielded in 1950, basically the legacy of Branch Rickey and the guts of the 1949 pennant-winning lineup, remained essentially intact for the next decade with Reese, Campanella, Snider, Hodges and Furillo holding down their positions until the Dodgers moved to Los Angeles in 1958. Reese and Robinson were the league's best base stealers, while Snider, Hodges and Campanella combined five times to hit over 100 homers in a season. Likewise, Billy Cox, Furillo, Snider, Reese, Robinson, Hodges and Campanella all took turns representing the best National League defense had to offer. This was one of the great National League teams of all time, one that took four pennants during the 1950s. So thorough was their domination of National League play that despite a lack of depth in their pitching staff, if the Dodgers had won a total of 19 more games from 1946-56, during which they took six flags and finished second three times, they could have won 11 pennants in 11 years.

Casey Stengel also fielded essentially the same Yankee team in 1950 that took the American League pennant in 1949, and again just managed to edge the Red Sox to log his second consecutive pennant. The usually dependable DiMaggio was clearly past his prime, but young talented southpaw Whitey Ford supplied the winning edge, taking nine out of ten games after he was brought up from the Yankees' Kansas City farm team.

Much credit for the Yankees' eight pennants in the 1950s must go to manager Stengel's fine-tuning of the Yankees' farm system. Departing from Rickey's assembly line approach, Stengel instead concen-

LEFT: *Two legends collide as Pee Wee Reese forces Willie Mays at second and throws while airborne to make the double play.*

BELOW LEFT: *Hall of Fame catcher Roy Campanella gets the throw in time to thwart Athletics first baseman Ferris Fain's attempt to steal home in the second inning of the 1951 All-Star game.*

trated on the most talented young players, in 1951 founding an 'instruction school' staffed by experts such as Bill Dickey and Frank Crosetti. The 1951 school, held in Phoenix, Arizona, graduated such pupils as 18-year-old Mickey Mantle, Gil McDougald and Tom Morgan. American League Rookies of the Year Bob Grim (1954) and Tony Kubek (1957) also moved directly into the majors from Casey's courses. Insisting that 'people alter percentages,' Stengel often relied on his extensive knowledge of both his opponents and his own players to fly in the face of established procedure, putting southpaw pitcher against lefthanded batter, for instance, when

the situation warranted it, with legendary results.

In 1950 it was the Phillies who made all the noise in the National League. Delaware millionaire Bob Carpenter had built up a young team, dubbed the 'Whiz Kids' for their youth and spirit, by investing heavily in the postwar bonus boom. The pennant race went down to the wire when some of the Whiz Kids suffered late-season injuries, and on 10 October Robin Roberts, the Phillies' first 20-game winner since 1917, faced Brooklyn's Don Newcombe in a game he had to win to protect the pennant from the Dodgers. It was Roberts' third start in five days. He and Newcombe remained deadlocked at 1-1 until

LEFT: *Robin Evan Roberts fires one to the plate in this 1956 photo. Roberts pitched for the Phillies from 1948 to 1961, logging six consecutive 20-win seasons beginning in 1950 and leading the league in wins from 1952 to 1955, four years during which he averaged better than 24 wins per season.*

BELOW: *Dick Sisler, son of immortal first baseman George Sisler, made history of his own on 1 October 1950 when his three-run homer in the top of the tenth saved the pennant for the Phillies. Exuberant teammates mobbed him after he crossed the plate. Despite an amazing season, the 'Whiz Kids' proved no match for the more experienced Yankees, who swept them in the Series.*

Dick Sisler, son of immortal George Sisler, who was then the Dodgers' chief scout, hit a three-run homer in the tenth to hand Philadelphia its first pennant in 35 years. The Whiz Kids, facing 'men who smoke cigars and chew tobacco,' went down four straight against the Yankees in the Series, although the games were all very close.

At the 27 February 1951 celebration of the National League's seventy-fifth anniversary in New York, a telegram from President Truman commending 'our national pastime' included the following observation:

> The founders of the National League and the fans of that era never dreamed the game would achieve such popularity or there would be such inventions as radio and television to carry it to millions of Americans all over the world.

They probably never dreamed that there would be an American League either, or a man named Bill Veeck, who purchased the St Louis Browns and in 1951 hired contortionist Max Patkin to clown on the coaching lines. Promotional artist Veeck also sent midget Eddie Gaedel to bat against Detroit in 1951. At three feet, seven inches Gaedel was impossible to pitch to and was walked in his only at bat. His career was cut short by league president Will Harridge, however, who was not amused. Veeck's many bizarre promotions, usually successful, roundly criticized at the time and later widely imitated, demonstrated that at least one club owner made no bones about the relationship between entertainment and baseball.

On the serious playing field 1951 was a year of remarkable rookie appearances. For the Yankees, who clinched their third straight pennant with help from Allie Reynolds' two no-hitters, 1951 was the last season for Joe DiMaggio but the first for Mickey Mantle, called up during the season, and for Gil McDougald, who led the team with a .306 average and became the only rookie to hit a grand slam home run in World Series play. In the National League, Rookie of the Year Willie Mays came up from the Giants' Minneapolis farm club in May and figured prominently in the Giants' remarkable end-of-season streak, which saw them take 16 games in a row – 37 of their final 44 games – to close the gap on the Dodgers.

The Giants were stopped from taking the pennant on the final day of the regular season by a legendary performance from Jackie Robinson, who almost singlehandedly, offensively and defensively, took a hard-fought game from the Phillies that forced the Dodgers and the Giants into a three-game playoff. In the bottom of the ninth in the third and deciding game of the series, Bobby Thomson hit the game-winning and pennant-clinching home run for the Giants which, known ever since as the 'Home Run Heard 'Round the World,' has come to symbolize ninth-inning diehard hopes.

Late-inning dramatics in the pennant race didn't help the Giants much in the Series against the Yankees, however. After dropping two games, the Bombers won in six to log their third consecutive world championship under Casey Stengel.

BELOW: *Midget Eddie Gaedel, here having his shoelaces tied by Browns manager Zack Taylor. The 26-year-old, 3-foot 7-inch midget was hired as a publicity stunt by Browns owner Bill Veeck in 1951 and came to the plate in a game against Detroit. He was walked in his only at-bat.*

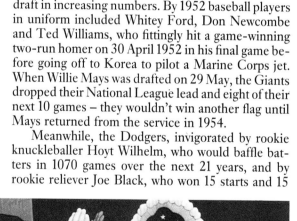

ABOVE: *Yankees batter Gil McDougald waits for the first pitch of the sixth game of the 1952 World Series. Billy Loes is pitching for the Dodgers and Roy Campanella is behind the plate. The Yankees won in seven.*

BELOW: *Twenty-one-year-old Willie Mays is sworn into the US Army on 29 May 1952 by Capt William F Donegan, Jr. The Giants' fortunes fell while their star outfielder served his country and rose when he returned.*

saves in 1952, came on strong to take back-to-back pennants in 1952 and 1953. Nineteen fifty-two was the year the Dodgers set a modern major league record by scoring 15 runs in the first inning of a game against the Reds – 19 of 21 Brooklyn batters reached base safely that inning.

The Yankee club the Bums faced in the Series had also suffered losses to the draft, but 20-year-old switch-hitter Mickey Mantle, batting .311, contributed 33 homers to help his team take the pennant from the Indians by two games. In the seventh game of the hard-fought Series Mantle knocked a deciding homer out of the park, and the New York Yankees and Casey Stengel recorded their fourth consecutive world championship.

The Babe Ruth League, for boys 13 to 15, was founded in 1952, but it was neither the first nor the largest of America's youth leagues. Its founding, rather, represents the flowering of youth league baseball in the 1950s and 1960s, a continuing development which undoubtedly contributes to the seemingly inexhaustible abundance of skilled youngsters coming up to the majors.

Although in America youth leagues have come to be known generically as 'Little League,' the Little League, founded by Carl E Stolz of Williamsport, Pennsylvania, in 1939, is one of several youth leagues. Stolz's idea, designed for boys 8 to 12 years of age, was well received, but had to wait until after World War II to make any real progress. Sixty Little League teams competed for a place in the 1947 Little League World Series, but by 1948 there were 416 teams, a number which nearly doubled in 1949 and continued growing at an astronomical pace until today there are some 145,000 teams in over 14,000 leagues worldwide. In 1964 Little League ball received a federal charter (although it receives no government funds), and in 1974 Congress approved another act which guarantees girls a chance to participate in Little League teams.

The first youth league in America, the American Legion Junior League, was founded in 1925 for teenagers up to age 17. It still survives and thrives as the American Legion League in every state and American protectorate, as does the American Amateur Baseball Congress, with five divisions for different age groups; the Pony League; the Colt League; and many other divisions and leagues across the country which all together give opportunities for over one million youngsters a year to play ball. Not to be forgotten are the 15,000-odd American junior high and high schools that sponsor at least one baseball team annually, affording many more youths the opportunity to play. While the goal of youth baseball is not specifically to prepare boys for baseball careers, 50 percent of active major league players in any given year have played in Little League, American Legion or related programs.

Mickey Mantle continued to make news in 1953 when he knocked a ball outside of Griffith Stadium in Washington, DC on 17 April. Alert Yankee press agent Red Patterson found a tape measure and when the next day's papers carried the news that Mantle had hit the ball 565 feet, the tape-measure home run was born. Also scoring in the superlative department

War had broken out in Korea in 1950, and while at first only regular American forces were involved, as the war dragged on American men found themselves called up through their reserve units or a reinstated draft in increasing numbers. By 1952 baseball players in uniform included Whitey Ford, Don Newcombe and Ted Williams, who fittingly hit a game-winning two-run homer on 30 April 1952 in his final game before going off to Korea to pilot a Marine Corps jet. When Willie Mays was drafted on 29 May, the Giants dropped their National League lead and eight of their next 10 games – they wouldn't win another flag until Mays returned from the service in 1954.

Meanwhile, the Dodgers, invigorated by rookie knuckleballer Hoyt Wilhelm, who would baffle batters in 1070 games over the next 21 years, and by rookie reliever Joe Black, who won 15 starts and 15

ABOVE: *Dodgers rookie Joe Black as he hurls his club to a 4-2 victory over the Yankees in the 1952 World Series, the Dodgers' first opening-game win in six World Series.*

LEFT: *A Little Leaguer takes a swing. In any given year, approximately 50 percent of active players in the major leagues are former players in organized youth league baseball.*

ABOVE: *Mickey Mantle slams a 565-foot homer out of Griffith Stadium, 17 April 1953. It was measured by a press agent, and the tape-measure homer was born.*

RIGHT: *Mantle is greeted by teammate Yogi Berra as he crosses the plate after hitting the longest ball ever hit, at Griffith Stadium.*

OPPOSITE LEFT: *The headline says it all. The Sox got 11 singles, 2 doubles, 1 homer and 6 walks for 17 runs in one 48-minute inning at Fenway.*

OPPOSITE TOP RIGHT: *Vice-President Richard M Nixon throws out the first ball for the new Baltimore Orioles, 15 April 1954.*

OPPOSITE RIGHT SEQUENCE: *Billy Martin hits a single driving Hank Bauer home to win the game and Series for the Yanks, 1953.*

were the Red Sox, who on 18 June set a new major league record by scoring an incredible 17 runs in one inning against the Detroit Tigers. But perhaps the news of greatest significance for baseball in 1953, including the Yankees' unprecedented fifth consecutive world championship, was the announcement, on 18 March, of a National League franchise shift – the first major league franchise shift in 53 years.

After years of declining attendance since their 1948 pennant-winning season, the Boston Braves moved to Milwaukee in 1953. Attendance for their first 13 games in Milwaukee was greater than their yearly total for 1952, and total 1953 attendance was greater than the 1948 pennant year total of 1,455,439. For the four years from 1954 to 1957, home attendance topped two million annually. Significantly, behind this show of support the Milwaukee Braves moved from near the bottom of the league to near the top, and with 23 wins from Warren Spahn and 47 homers from Eddie Mathews finished second to the overpowering Dodgers, with whom they traded first and second place from 13 May onward.

Ted Williams hit .407 after returning from Korea to the Red Sox lineup on 6 August, but with Mickey Mantle sparking his club to an 18-game winning streak the Yankees finished eight and a half games ahead of the Indians to take their fifth consecutive pennant. New York then took its fifth consecutive Series in six games, although Brooklyn's Carl Erskine struck out fourteen Yankees in the third game for a new World Series record.

d Sox' 17-Run Inning
Shakes 16 Major Marks

tephens' Three
Hits New Record;
e on Base 3 Times

HY HURWITZ

BOSTON, Mass.

the weakest hitting
ecent Red Sox history
the greatest batting
modern times when
reau's men racked up
inning while wallop-
igers, 23 to 3, at Fen-
k, June 18.
ing a 17 to 1 trouncing
it the previous day,
ox, who collected 14 hits
sses in the 17-run inning,
one all-time major
ord and tied eight others,
ern marks and one Amer-
ue standard in the one
round.
the most fantastic indi-
rks—three hits in one in-
20-year-old Gene Steph-
entered the game with a
ng average, almost didn't
nly for the fact that Man-
Boudreau had one spare
left—Hoot Evers, who was
lame back—was Stephens
to go to bat a third time
toric seventh.
d put on an amazing burst
in his second time at bat
g to stretch a routine sin-
a double. He had hit a
rounder between first and
d directly at Right Fielder
san. He legged it for sec-
nade it, but in the process
omething in his neck.

• • •

ne Ignores Injury

ene, stiff neck and all.
bat for a third time and
rough with a sizzling
to right field. No mod-
er had ever made three
he same inning.
the Sox sent 23 batters
late, only four modern
ad gone to bat three times
me frame since 1900. The
o do it was Ted Williams of
Sox against the Philadelphia

Boston Massacre in Figures

AMERICAN LEAGUE											
P		1	2	3	4	5	6	7	8	9	H
35	DETROIT	0	0	0	2	0	1	0			4
16	BOSTON	0	3	0	0	0	2	17			24
33	ST. LOUIS	0									0
18	NEW YORK	0									5

THE STORY ON THE SCOREBOARD AT FENWAY PARK

Freddy Hatfield of the Tigers being the leading principals in a battle of vicious insults. The Sox were
steaming mad at the remarks passed
on to Piersall by Batts and Hatfield.
Piersall got in the final word when
he broke up a 3 to 3 tie in the sixth
with a two-run single and singled
home two runs in the seventh.
Manager Lou Boudreau removed
Piersall from the game when Jim
was due to bat for a second time.

Hi-Jinks in Hub

Following are the records set and
tied during the game, with the previous record holder shown in paren-
theses:

All-Time Major League Record Set
Most runs batted in, inning, one
club—17—Red Sox (15, Chicago vs.
Detroit N. L., September 6, 1883, seventh inning; Brooklyn vs. Cincinnati
N. L., May 21, 1952, first inning. Former A. L. record — 14 — Boston vs.
Philadelphia, July 4, 1948, seventh inning.)

All-Time Major League Records Tied
Most batters facing pitcher, inning,
one club—23—Red Sox (Chicago vs.
Detroit N. L., September 6, 1883, seventh inning. Former A. L. record—
19—Boston vs. Philadelphia, July 4,
1948, seventh inning.)
Most batters facing pitcher three
times, inning, one club—5—Red Sox;
Sam White, Gene Stephens, Tom
Umphlett, Johnny Lipon and George
Kell (Chicago vs. Detroit N. L., September 6, 1883, seventh inning; Edward N. Williamson, Thomas E. Burns,
Edward N. Pfeffer, Fred E. Goldsmith
and William A. Sunday. Former A. L.
record—1—Boston vs. Philadelphia,
July 4, 1948, seventh inning.)

SAMMY WHITE crossing
the plate with run No. 17.

Long, Robert L. Lowe and Hugh Duffy, Boston N. L., June 18, 1894, morn-
ing game, first inning. Harold H.
Reese, Brooklyn, May 21, 1952, first
inning. Former A. L. record—2—held

After the season Dodgers manager Charlie Dres-
sen, with two consecutive pennants under his belt,
made the mistake of formulating his demand for a
three-year contract in terms of an ultimatum. The
Dodgers organization, which preferred one-year
contracts, replaced him with Montreal manager
Walter Alston, who eventually signed 23 one-year
contracts with the Dodgers. St Louis Browns owner
Bill Veeck, twice refused permission to move his
financially troubled club, primarily because the other
owners wanted this unconventional troublemaker out
of baseball, was finally permitted to sell his franchise
to a syndicate which moved it to Baltimore, where it
became the Orioles in 1954. The lessons of the
Braves' success had clearly not been lost on the
owners; these two franchise shifts were not to be
isolated occurrences. The Athletics moved to Kansas
City for the 1955 season. Both the Athletics and the
Orioles drew well in their initial season and steadily
rising profits ensured that the trend would continue.

Most of the ballplayers who had gone into the service to fight in Korea were back in the game for the
1954 season. Among them was Willie Mays, whose
MVP performance – 41 home runs, 110 RBIs and a
league-leading .345 average – spirited the Giants to
their first pennant since his departure in 1951. Teammate Don Mueller seconded his batting average, and
Johnny Antonelli contributed 21 wins. Milwaukee
slugger Joe Adcock hit four homers and a double for
the most bases in a single game; and Stan Musial hit
five homers in a double-header to set a new major

league record. In an event that would take on considerably greater significance in retrospect, a rookie named Henry Aaron hit his first major league home run on 23 April 1954.

The brand new Orioles lost 100 games in their inaugural season, despite a sensational opening day parade and a benediction from Vice-President Nixon; and the Yankees, who won 103 games, were edged in the American League by a Cleveland squad with 111 wins – the 1927 Yanks had previously held the American League season record of 110 wins. Indian manager Al Lopez, who had played under Stengel in the National League, had solid hitters in Al Rosen and Bobby Avila, but superb pitching in Bob Lemon and Early Wynn, both 23-game winners, Mike Garcia with 18 wins, and Bob Feller, still good for a 13-3 season.

The Indians were expected to take the Giants in the Series, but instead the Giants swept the Indians for the first National League Series win since 1949 and the first National League Series sweep since 1914. To many, the National League sweep was evidence that the National League had become baseball's power center. A significant factor in this shift, still evident today, was the Senior Circuit's less cautious attitude in signing blacks. The Yankees, for instance, didn't play their first black, Elston Howard, until the 1954 season. The Red Sox didn't sign a black until 1959, thereby depriving themselves of bidding on a fine pool of talent.

Although Willie Mays claims he has made much more difficult plays – even in the same game – the catch he made off Vic Wertz in the eighth inning of the first game of the Series, ensuring a Giants victory, will be remembered as long as he is. With the score

tied at 2-2, Mays started running on Wertz's swing and continued running at full speed with his back to the plate until the ball fell into his upturned glove 10 feet from the center-field fence. Before he went sprawling he managed to rifle a throw to the infield that prevented the runner on second from taking more than one base.

Ninety-two-year-old Connie Mack appeared for the opening game of the brand new Kansas City Athletics' 1955 season. The move that marked the beginning of the American League's western expansion didn't bring the Athletics much luck, however, as they finished out of contention. The Yankees, despite outstanding pitching from Cleveland's Herb Score, took the pennant in a tight race between the Indians, White Sox and Red Sox.

It was a different story for the Dodgers team that would face the Yankees in the Series for the third time in four years. Beginning with 22 wins out of their first 24 games, the 1955 Bums controlled first place after one month, never lost it, and clinched the pennant on 8 September, the earliest date in National League history. Carrying their momentum into the world championship, they took the Series in seven games, thanks in part to a legendary catch by Sandy Amoros in the sixth inning of the seventh game that squelched a dangerous Yankee rally. This was the first world championship ever for the Dodgers. As fate and franchise shift would have it, it was also the only world championship the Brooklyn Dodgers would ever win.

Nineteen fifty-six, the year the National League made it compulsory for all players to wear protective headgear while batting, will always be remembered as the year that Ted Williams spat at jeering fans and

ABOVE: *Elston Gene 'Ellie' Howard signed on with the Yankees in 1955 and played most of his 14-year career in the majors behind the plate and in the outfield, appearing in nine World Series with the Yanks and one in 1967 with the Red Sox, with whom he played his last year and a half. He was the first black signed to the New York Yankees.*

RIGHT: *Yankees pitcher Don Larsen throws the third strike past Dodgers pinch hitter Dale Mitchell for the last out in the only perfect World Series game, 8 October 1956. Billy Martin stands poised at second base; the scoreboard tells the story.*

BOTTOM: *The great Mickey Mantle, 'The Commerce Comet,' began his 18-year career with the Yankees in 1951. He led the league in home runs four times, in runs scored six times, and in batting and RBIs once. He collected three MVPs, including the Triple Crown in his 1956 MVP year, and helped put the Yankees in 12 World Series during his 18-year tenure.*

was fined $5000. In a development that would have somewhat more far-reaching effects, the Major League Baseball Players' Association was formally organized at the end of the season. Attempts to form a real players' union were almost as old as professional baseball; the new union would soon become a powerful force in organized ball.

Although the Yankees were on top again at All-Star break, the White Sox, a young, aggressive team featuring Luis Aparacio, Minnie Minoso, Jim Rivera, Nellie Fox, Larry Doby and Sherman Lollar, gave the Bombers plenty to worry about. An outstanding year from young Mickey Mantle, however, who became the fourth man in baseball history to lead both leagues in homers (53), RBIs (130) and batting average (.353) turned the trick for New York, and for the fourth time in the 1950s the Bombers met the Bums in the Series.

Don Newcombe won the first Cy Young Award and took his twenty-seventh win on the final day of the 1956 season, a win Brooklyn desperately needed to preserve their pennant from a threatening Milwaukee club that would take pennants in 1957 and 1958. But in 1956 the Dodgers once again earned the right to face the Yankees in the last of their epic Subway Series. The Yankees' victory in seven, however, will always be overshadowed by the pitching duel in the fifth game between Brooklyn's Sal Maglie and New York's Don Larsen. Mickey Mantle ended

Maglie's no-hitter with a home run in the fourth, but Larsen's game continued without a hit and he came into the ninth inning having faced only 24 batters, working on a perfect game. Furillo flied out and Campanella grounded out, leaving Larsen one out away from an unprecedented achievement. When umpire Babe Pinelli called a third strike on Dale Mitchell, Larsen had done it – he had pitched the first and only perfect game in World Series history.

Spirited by Warren Spahn's eighth 20-win season and solid pitching from Lew Burdette and Bob Buhl, not to mention MVP Henry Aaron's 44 homers, 132 RBIs and .322 average, the Braves, who in their fifth year in Milwaukee also featured the slugging of Eddie Mathews and veterans Joe Adcock and Red Schoendienst, returned the warm reception their new town had given them by topping the league in 1957, putting the Dodgers in third place after St Louis. It was the first time the Bums finished out of first or second place in nine years. In the American League the Indians would have given the Yankees a better run for their money except for a tragic accident on 7 May, when Gil McDougald lined a ball into young pitching phenomenon Herb Score's right eye. Score was able to return to baseball, but without the stuff that had won him 16 and 20 games during his first two years, during which he had also led the league in strikeouts.

BELOW: *Dodgers left fielder Sandy Amoros making his famous one-handed catch of Yankee Yogi Berra's long ball in the 1955 World Series. Amoros ran 100 feet to make his amazing catch and got it to the infield via Pee Wee Reese fast enough to double up Gil McDougald, saving the final game and the Series for the Dodgers, their first and only World Series win in Brooklyn.*

ABOVE: *Fans chase the Giants into the clubhouse after the last game at the Polo Grounds, 30 September 1957, as the Pirates trot up the steps to the left. Citing declining attendance, the Giants announced they were moving to San Francisco at the close of the 1957 season.*

The Braves, who set a new National League attendance record of 2,215,404 during the regular 1957 season, crowned their glorious year by taking the World Series from the Yankees in seven, thanks largely to a superb effort from Lew Burdette, whose three Series wins included two shutouts. Ted Williams, at 39, became the oldest American Leaguer to take a batting title (Stan Musial led the National League for the seventh time with .351). Williams batted .388 in 1957 and took the title again in 1958, although with a more human .328 average.

Record-breaking numbers of fans showing up at the ballparks in the late 1950s indicated that organized ball was hitting one of its periodic peaks of popularity. With television creating a national mar-

ket, it was only a matter of time before the majors considered expanding to the prosperous West Coast. The Milwaukee Braves' enviable attendance figures no doubt confirmed the owners' belief that greener pastures were attainable. Declining attendance in antiquated parks in deteriorating urban settings was the last straw. At the close of the 1957 season the Giants, citing declining attendance, announced that they were moving to San Francisco, and the Dodgers, citing inadequate facilities, announced that they were forsaking Brooklyn for Los Angeles. Giant president Horace Stoneham, when asked if he didn't feel badly about taking the Giants away from New York kids, delivered the classic, 'I feel bad about the kids, but I haven't seen too many of their fathers lately.'

TOP RIGHT: *Yankee Yogi Berra catches the ball barehanded as Milwaukee's Wes Covington scores on Johnny Logan's single in the first inning of the second Series game of 1958.*

RIGHT: *Edwin Lee 'Eddie' Mathews held down third base for the Braves from 1952 to 1966 in Boston, Milwaukee and Atlanta, compiling a career batting average of .271 and 512 lifetime home runs.*

RIGHT: *Chicago White Sox manager Al Lopez shouts in relief as his team gets the final out against the Indians in the bottom of the ninth. The 2-0 Chicago victory over Cleveland on 29 August 1959 gave the Sox a three and a half game lead in the American League pennant race. Lopez would skipper his club to its first Series appearance since 1919.*

BELOW: *Harvey Haddix of the Pirates on the evening of 26 May 1959 when he pitched the eighth perfect game recorded since 1876. Haddix then kept the Braves scoreless for three more innings, becoming the first pitcher ever to retire 28 men in a row, the first to pitch a perfect game for more than nine innings, and the first to pitch a no-hitter for more than eleven innings.*

Thanks to 20-win years from Warren Spahn and Lew Burdette, the Milwaukee Braves repeated in 1958, while the Los Angeles Dodgers, despite record attendance, plunged to seventh place. The San Francisco Giants, with outstanding performances from Willie Mays and rookie Orlando Cepeda, came in third. The Yankees repeated in the American League for their fourth consecutive flag, bringing their pennant total to nine flags in ten years. In the Series rematch the defending Braves worked up a 3-1 lead before Yankees Gil McDougald and Bill Skowron came through with timely homers in the fifth, sixth and seventh games to return the World Championship once again to New York.

By May 1959, however, the seemingly unstoppable 'damn' Yankees, plagued by slumps and injuries, were actually at the bottom of their league; they finished the season out of contention, that year's American League race taking place between the White Sox and the Indians. The White Sox, managed by Al Lopez, who had formerly managed the Indians, combined solid pitching, speed and a strong defense to beat the Indians by five games, thereby earning the right to face the Los Angeles Dodgers, who had overcome a two-game Giant lead in the final week and bested the Braves in the National League's third pennant playoff. The Dodgers took the Series in six, meanwhile breaking all attendance records for single

Series games in their second year at the Los Angeles Coliseum, where 92,796 spectators paid to see the third Series match.

The Red Sox finally signed a black player – Elijah 'Pumpsie' Green – in 1959, becoming the last major league club to do so and reminding those who thought that Jackie Robinson had thrown some kind of magic switch in 1947, ending racism and integrating baseball, that the path to true racial equality was in fact somewhat more tortuous. But the closing year of the decade will be remembered perhaps more than anything else for Harvey Haddix's 12-inning perfect game – which he lost.

Pittsburgh's Haddix had a relatively undistinguished record when he faced Lew Burdette and the Braves on 29 May, but he managed to retire 27 Braves in nine innings – including the likes of Aaron, Mathews and Adcock – and nine more in three extra innings before Mantilla reached base on a Pirate fielding error, Aaron walked, and Adcock hit a home run to end the game in the thirteenth inning.

The pastures encountered by the franchises that had changed towns in the 1950s turned out to be so green and the popularity of baseball reached such a peak by the end of the decade that Branch Rickey, attorney William A Shea and others decided the time was ripe for a third major league, to be called the Continental League. Controversy surrounding its formation at times overshadowed play on the field during 1959, as did Congressional hearings into the laws governing baseball. In the end, due largely to the failure of a bill sponsored by Senator Estes Kefauver to pass Congress, the Continental League was stillborn; but on 2 August 1960 Shea and Rickey announced that the existing major leagues would absorb their franchises.

LEFT: *Pirates manager Danny Murtaugh shakes the hand of pitcher Harvey Haddix as he walks off the mound in the thirteenth inning. Haddix not only threw the best-pitched game in baseball history – he lost it in the thirteenth inning, when Felix Mantilla became the first of 37 batters Haddix faced to get on base (on a fielding error). Mathews bunted Mantilla to second, Aaron was intentionally walked, and Joe Adcock knocked his second pitch over the fence to drive in the runners. The Pirates never scored.*

ABOVE: *Seventy-seven-year-old president of the Continental League Branch Rickey hurls Commissioner Ford Frick's words back at him. Speaking to newsmen in his hotel suite on 29 October 1959, Rickey came close to a direct charge of bad faith as he called upon Frick and other baseball officials to honor their 'unqualified assurance' of support for a third league.*

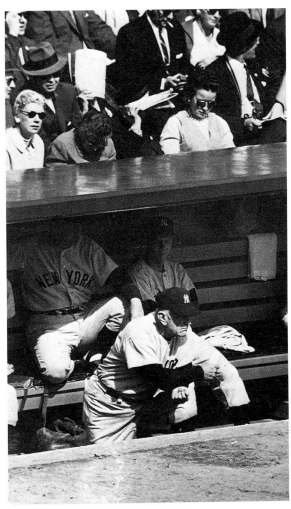

Meanwhile, on the field, Ted Williams took over third place from Mel Ott in lifetime home runs with number 512 on 10 August 1960. Williams would end his career that season with a .316 average and hit his twenty-ninth home run of the season in his final at bat. The Yankees once more asserted their dominance in the American League to hand Casey Stengel his tenth pennant in twelve years with the club, a win that tied him for most league championships with manager John McGraw.

In the National League the Pirates surprised everyone and earned their first Series appearance since 1927, when they had also faced the Yankees. In 1927 the Yankees had taken them in four games; this time the Yankees out-hit the Pirates 91 to 60 and out-scored them 55 to 27, delivering a humiliating 12-0 shutout in the sixth game, the widest shutout margin in Series history. But the Bucs managed to put their runs in the right places. In the seventh and deciding game Pirate Bill Mazeroski, whose homer had provided the margin in the first game, blasted a Ralph Terry fastball out of Forbes Field in the bottom of the ninth to win the Series for the Pirates and gain immortality for himself with what has been called the most timely home run in World Series history.

Mickey Mantle sat down in the locker room and cried after the game. The loss also cost Casey Stengel his job. When told he was too old, the Great Casey commented, 'I'll never make the mistake of being 70 years old again.' But as much as anything else his firing marked the end of a golden age of baseball, of an exciting era of superb play which left numerous unforgettable moments and set the stage for a new decade of expansion.

OPPOSITE: *Pittsburgh Pirate Bill Mazeroski is joined by third base coach Frank Oceak and triumphant fans as he heads for the plate after hitting a home run in the bottom of the ninth inning in the seventh game of the 1960 World Series. The blast gave the Pirates the game and the Series over the Yanks. It was Pittsburgh's first World Championship in 35 years.*

LEFT: *Yankees manager Casey Stengel watches glumly as the Pirates take an early lead in the first game of the 1960 World Series. Stengel lost his job after the Pirates won the Series in seven games.*

BELOW: *The great Ted Williams goes out in style, slamming a home run in his last major league at-bat. He hit 29 homers and averaged .316 in 1960, his nineteenth and last season with the Red Sox.*

CHAPTER SIX
A Decade of Expansion

While the world and the nation rocked to the changes of the 1960s – the assassination of President Kennedy, the agony of Vietnam, the 'expanded consciousness' of the drug culture – baseball remained relatively calm. The primary expansion organized ball experienced during the decade was the addition by both major leagues of more teams, a development which, given the exceptional popularity of baseball during the 1950s, the demographic shifts in the United States to the West and the Southwest, and the creation of a national audience via the medium of TV, was inevitable anyway. The threatened formation of the Continental League had only hastened the process. And while it is true that baseball has always reflected the larger patterns in American society, even in the case of integration, in which baseball took the lead, it was over a decade before all major teams were integrated. So it was that it would take another decade before baseball recapitulated the profound attitudinal and social changes of the 1960s.

Nineteen sixty-one was a watershed year for major league baseball in several ways. Not only were teams added to a major league for the first time since 1901, but in so doing, eight extra games were added to the expanded American League schedule. The 1961 season began with two new American League teams: the Minnesota Twins, in Minneapolis, and the Angels, in Los Angeles, whose name became the California Angels in 1966. The Twins were actually the Washington Senators moved to Minneapolis; a new franchise took over in Washington and retained the name of Senators. When the National League added the Mets in New York City and the Colt 45s in Houston in 1962 (their name changed to the Astros in 1965), the Senior Circuit also expanded to a 162-game season, a move that immediately became controversial.

OPPOSITE: *Don Mincher of the Minnesota Twins connects for a solo home run in the second inning of the 1965 World Series opener. Dodgers pitcher Don Drysdale stares skyward forlornly. Minnesota's big bats took the first game, but the Dodgers took the Series in seven.*

RIGHT: *United States President John F Kennedy throws out the first ball at the All-Star game, 10 July 1962.*

ABOVE: *Yankee Roger Maris belts his sixty-first home run of 1961. Never as charismatic or as popular as Babe Ruth, whose record he broke, Maris found his achievement marred by the reaction of fans who didn't want to see Ruth's record broken, and by fans who would have preferred to see the record broken by his more popular teammate, Mickey Mantle.*

RIGHT: *Yankee Mickey Mantle connects for a home run at Forbes Field in the second game of the 1960 World Series. Always outstanding in Series play, Mantle hit two in this game to spur New York to a 16-3 victory over the Pirates. When he retired in 1968, he led the majors in total Series homers.*

FAR LEFT: *Milwaukee's Warren Spahn as he pitches a two-hitter against the New York Yankees in the fourth game of the 1958 World Series. He shut out the Yanks, 3-0, but the Yankees took the Series in seven games.*

LEFT: *Yankees ace Whitey Ford begins his delivery in the 1961 World Series opener against the Reds. Ford was a league-leading 25-4 during the regular 1961 season. He shut out the Reds 2-0 in this game, his third consecutive scoreless Series effort and eighth Series win.*

For 1961 was the year that the Yankees' 'M & M Boys,' Mickey Mantle and Roger Maris, mounted a two-pronged assault on Babe Ruth's season record of 60 home runs. Jimmie Foxx had banged out 58 in 1932 and Hank Greenberg had equalled him in 1938 (Hack Wilson's 56 is still the National League record), but no one had yet equalled the Babe, whose record was considered so sacrosanct in some quarters that no one wanted it to be equalled or surpassed. Hank Aaron would run up against similar reverential feelings for Babe Ruth's records when he approached the Babe's lifetime home run total in the early 1970s.

Despite an excellent start Mantle was prevented by injuries from hitting more than 54 home runs in 1961. Teammate Elston Howard once remarked that if Mantle had been able to stay healthy for an entire season, he would have hit 70 home runs. The honor instead fell to the much less charismatic Roger Maris, who got his sixtieth homer by his 154th game but didn't hit number 61 until game 162. Commissioner Ford Frick had previously ruled that Ruth's record would remain special unless topped within the 154 games of the pre-expansion circuit; purists satisfied themselves that Ruth's 60 homers in 1927 amounted to 14 percent of his league's season home run output while Maris's 61 represented only four percent. Maris's mark went into the record books with an asterisk.

Lest 1961 be remembered only for its home runs, it should be mentioned that on 28 April of the season the great Warren Spahn pitched the second no-hitter of his career against the San Francisco Giants. At 40 years of age, Spahn was just a bit younger than Cy Young, the oldest man to pitch a no-hitter, who was 41 when he pitched his third on 20 June 1908. Spahn, whose endurance and skill recalled the greats of old, would record a 23-7 year in 1963, when he was 42; he had also had a 23-7 year in 1953.

Behind the slugging of the M & M Boys, the Yankees dominated the American League and handed new manager Ralph Houk his first flag, the second of five consecutive pennants the Bombers would take in the first five years of the decade. In the process of downing the Reds in the Series, 4-1, another Babe Ruth record fell as Whitey Ford passed his long-standing mark of 29 and two-thirds innings and completed a victorious 1961 Series appearance with 32 consecutive scoreless innings.

Casey Stengel and general manager George Weiss, who had lost their heads in the Yankee organization in 1960 when the club failed to take the Series from the Pirates, skippered the 1962 National League expansion club the Mets to 120 losses in their maiden season, a major league record that has yet to be equalled. In the American League the Angels and the Twins, both in their second season, gave the Yankees a good run for the money, especially the Twins, whose heavy hitting would push them to the top of the league in 1965.

ABOVE: *Yankees second baseman Bobby Richardson throws toward first after making the force on San Francisco's Orlando Cepeda, sliding with spikes high, in the third game of the 1962 Series.*

RIGHT: *Los Angeles Dodger Maury Wills slides into base. In 1962 Wills tied Ty Cobb's 47-year-old record of 96 stolen bases in 156 games and set a new major league record of 104. In his first seven years in the majors, he led the National League in stolen bases six times.*

Still, 1962 was the Yankees' year, and the Bombers met the Giants in the Series after the San Francisco club downed New York's other arch-enemy, the Dodgers, in an exciting three-game playoff for the National League pennant. The evenly matched World Series also went down to the wire, into the bottom of the ninth inning of the seventh game, when with the Yankees leading 1-0 and two outs the Giants got two men on base and hard-hitting Willie McCovey came to bat against Ralph Terry. Terry may or may not have recalled a similar situation in which he had pitched to Mazeroski two years previously, with disastrous results. This time, however, when McCovey connected for a solid liner second baseman Bobby Richardson made a memorable catch that saved the game and clinched the Series for New York.

More records fell in 1962. Fleet-footed Maury Wills of Los Angeles overtook Ty Cobb's 47-year-old record of 96 stolen bases and set a new major league season mark of 104. Stan Musial registered hit number 3431, taking over first place league honors in this department from Honus Wagner; and Sandy Koufax tied his own and Bob Feller's record of 18 strikeouts in nine innings, although a circulation problem in his pitching hand benched him in the second half of the season. Similar bad luck plagued aging pitcher Early Wynn, who finished the 1962 season one shy of the magic 300 lifetime wins. The

White Sox released him, then permitted him to report for spring training in 1963, but when they failed to sign him Wynn was taken in by his old club, the Cleveland Indians. Pitching with gout in his limbs and painkillers in his belly, he became the fourteenth major leaguer and the first American Leaguer since Lefty Grove to compile 300 lifetime wins, in a July game against Kansas City. In the Series, Whitey Ford ended his record consecutive scoreless championship innings at 33 and two-thirds.

Pitcher Camilo Pascual, who had won 20 games the year before, won 21 for the Twins in 1963, but the big news in Minnesota that year was the fledgling club's record-breaking display of power hitting, which saw their sluggers hit eight homers in the first game of a doubleheader and four in the second. Harmon Killebrew and Vic Power each hit a pair. But the Yankees were not to be denied. Not only did they repeat in the American League, they won by 10 and a half games, their largest margin since 1947. Significantly, they won despite injuries sustained by Mickey Mantle when he ran into a wall chasing a fly ball. The accident limited him to 65 games; Maris, plagued with back troubles, was limited to 90 games that year.

While Cincinnati Rookie of the Year Pete Rose looked on, Stan Musial ended his twenty-second year as a Cardinal and his career as a player by knocking out hit number 3630 and RBI number 1951 in his final at bat. His club gave the Dodgers some bad

ABOVE: *Twins first baseman Vic Power steals second in a May 1962 Minnesota-Detroit game as Tigers second baseman Steve Boros gloves a throw that came too late from the plate. Shortstop Chico Fernandez backs Boros up as umpire Al Smith makes the call.*

ABOVE: *Dodgers ace Don Drysdale unwinds in the ninth inning of a June 1968 Dodgers-Giants game at Candlestick Park on the way to his 200th major league win. Drysdale gave up only two hits in his 2-1 victory and had a no-hitter going for seven and two-thirds innings until a single by pinch hitter Dave Marshall drove in a Giants runner.*

ABOVE RIGHT: *Mel Stottlemyre shows his form in 1972. Stottlemyre played his entire major league career with the Yankees, 1964 to 1974, three times winning 20 games or better and compiling 164 lifetime wins.*

RIGHT: *Philadelphia's Jim Bunning throws strike three against San Diego's Clarence Gaston to record his 2820th strikeout, 31 May 1971, making him the second all-time strike-out pitcher behind Walter Johnson, with 3508.*

moments in their race to the pennant, but behind solid slugging from Frank Howard and Tommy Davis, fleet baserunning from Wills, Willie Davis and Jim Gilliam and the pitching of Drysdale, Podres and Koufax, even a 25-win season from San Francisco's Juan Marichal and a 21-win season from Milwaukee's Warren Spahn were not good enough. The powerhouse Dodgers went on to knock the Yankees out of the Series in the minimum of four games, demonstrating that the New Yorkers were not only not invincible but even human. Koufax logged two Series wins, breaking Carl Erskine's 1953 Series record by striking out 15 Yankees in the first game.

The great Yogi Berra made his last appearance as a player in game three of the 1963 Series, pinch-hitting without success for Jim Bouton, but re-appeared as the manager of the Yankees in 1964 (Houk moved up to general manager). Quoth Yogi, 'My big problem as manager will be to see if I can manage.' That season ace Yankee pitcher Whitey Ford developed a bad hip. The team got off to a slow start and languished in third place until out of desperation Berra brought pitcher Mel Stottlemyre up from the Richmond farm club in August. Stottlemyre's fine performance from his debut win on sparked the team and elicited solid performances from fellow pitchers Ford and Bouton and sluggers Mantle, Maris, Howard and Joe Pepitone that put the Yankees on top for their twenty-ninth pennant.

It was also their last of the decade. Strong new players coming up on other American League teams, particularly on the Orioles and the Red Sox, would put an end to Yankee dominance for some time to come. The Red Sox had rookie Tony Conigliaro, who hit 24 homers in 1964 despite a broken arm in July and led the league with 32 homers in 1965, as well as Dick 'The Monster' Radatz, who pitched in 79 and won 16 games in relief that year. Powerful John 'Boog' Powell hit 39 home runs for the Orioles in 1964. The Angels had pitcher Dean Chance and Jim Fregosi at short, the Indians had young Louis Tiant on the mound, and Kansas City had Bert Cam-

paneris to seal up the infield. This impressive assortment of talented players would combine to rewrite the American League map.

In National League play the Phillies, whose Jim Bunning logged the first of three consecutive 19-win seasons, including a perfect game (the first in modern National League baseball), appeared to have the pennant sewn up until their six and a half game lead evaporated to 10 straight losses in the final two weeks of the season. Meanwhile, the Cardinals, featuring the fastball of Bob Gibson, the base-stealing of Lou Brock and the solid hitting of Dick Groat, Ken Boyer, Bill White, Tim McCarver and Curt Flood won eight in a row to edge the Phillies by one game for the flag, earning the dubious privilege of facing a Yankee club fresh from its fifth straight flag in the Series. With Ford limited by a sore hip, Tony Kubek out with a sprained wrist and Mantle limping on a bad left leg, the contest seesawed back and forth for six games. In the seventh game, with Gibson facing Stottlemyre, Mantle's three-run homer in the sixth destroyed Gibson's 6-0 shutout, but two more homers from New York's Clete Boyer and Phil Linz was all she wrote, and St Louis hung on to take the game, 7-5, and the Series.

Age and injury stopped the Yankees from repeating in 1965. In fact, their sixth place finish was their lowest since 1925; but it opened up new possibilities for American League clubs that had played for so long in their shadow. The Minnesota Twins, formerly the lowly Washington Senators, managed by modest Sam Mele, battled their way to the top with their bats, taking their league's flag for the first time ever. Harmon Killebrew, Bob Allison, Don Mincher and Jimmie Hall hit the ball as hard as they could while Tony Oliva won the American League batting title with a .321 average and fielded well enough at short to earn the league's MVP Award. Jim 'Mudcat' Grant, after six uneventful years in Cleveland, turned in a 21-7 season in his first year with Minnesota. The rest of the Twins' pitchers were buoyed by their batsmen; the 1965 Twins were a hitters' team.

ABOVE LEFT: *Power-hitter John Wesley 'Boog' Powell played outfield and first base for Baltimore from 1961 to 1974, averaging 23 homers and 85 RBIs in five pennant seasons.*

ABOVE: *Dodgers great Sandy Koufax pitching against the Twins in the seventh game of the 1965 World Series. He shut them out, 2-0, to win the championship for Los Angeles.*

LEFT: *Bob Gibson of the St Louis Cardinals in action against the Mets, 13 April 1969. The Hall of Fame hurler won 22 games in 1968, 20 in 1969, and led the league with 23 in 1970.*

Willie Mays hit 52 home runs for the San Francisco Giants in 1965 and both his club and the Dodgers got so hot in September, winning 14 and 13 in a row, respectively, that the Cardinals found themselves out of their league. Pitching for the Dodgers, Sandy Koufax with a 26-8 season and Don Drysdale with 23-12 were simply overwhelming. Between them they struck out almost 600 hapless opponents, Koufax setting a new major league record of 382 season Ks that stood until Nolan Ryan bettered it by one in 1973. On 9 September Koufax pitched a perfect game against Bob Hendley of the Cubs in a pitchers' duel that saw Hendley give up only one hit and one run to the Dodgers. With pitching like this and hitting like the Twins', the World Series shaped up as a classic confrontation.

The Dodgers had in fact hit fewer home runs than any major league team in 1965, but relied for offense on steady hitting and savvy baserunning: Maury Wills hit only .286 but stole 94 bases. Since the Series opened in Minnesota on Yom Kippur, Sandy Koufax spent the day in religious observance and was unavailable to pitch; Don Drysdale faced the Twins' big bats. They shelled him for an 8-2 victory, and the next day they knocked Koufax off the mound for a 5-1 win, disheartening Dodgers fans with the rarity of defeating Drysdale and Koufax back-to-back. Back in Los Angeles, however, the Dodgers revived their strategy of singles, stolen bases and superb pitching to win three in a row. The pattern of home-team victories held as the Twins evened it up in the sixth, but in the seventh and deciding game, Koufax, pitching on two days' rest, shut the Twins down 2-0 despite a fine effort from Jim Kaat. It was the fourth World Championship for Dodgers manager Walter Alston.

LEFT: *Hall of Famer Frank Robinson of Baltimore takes a cut in the sixth game of the 1971 World Series with Pittsburgh. After 21 outstanding years as a player, Robinson became the first black manager in the major leagues, managing Cleveland from 1975 to 1977 and San Francisco from 1981 to 1984.*

BELOW: *Hall of Famer Brooks Robinson played for Baltimore for 23 years, teaming up with Frank Robinson for some of the Orioles' finest seasons. At his retirement in 1977, Brooks held all-time records for third basemen for fielding percentage, games played, putouts, assists and double plays.*

In 1966 the Baltimore Orioles, formerly the St Louis Browns, displayed the kind of stuff that would earn them four American League pennants in the next six years. By the end of July 1966 they had taken a 13-game lead that was never seriously challenged. Meanwhile, the mighty Yankees, still smarting from their sixth place finish of the previous season, sank to the bottom of the league. This was only the third time in the club's 64-year history that it had occupied this unenviable position. The replacement of 1965's manager Johnny Keane by Ralph Houk, author of former successes, was to no avail. In related developments, CBS purchased controlling interest in the club in mid-September and named Mike Burke president and Lee MacPhail, son of Larry MacPhail, general manager. Out on the Coast the California Angels moved into their new triple-decked stadium, which had been built for them in Anaheim in under two years at a cost of $24 million.

The Orioles owed their 1966 success to dependably strong seasons from Boog Powell, Luis Aparicio and Paul Blair, and particularly to the performances of their two Robinsons, Frank and Brooks. Brooks Robinson, who was the American League's 1964 MVP, had been with the Orioles since 1955 and would remain with them for his entire 23-year career. Always a strong hitter, in 1966 he began to receive popular recognition for a performance at third that established him as one of the all-time greats at his position and gained him admission into the Hall of Fame in 1983. The other Robinson, hard-hitting Frank, came to the Orioles in 1966 after he was let go by the National League's Cincinnati Reds because they thought he was asking for too much money. In his first year as an Oriole he led his new league in batting (.316), home runs (49) and RBIs (122) and was named American League MVP, thus becoming the only player to win the distinction in both leagues (he

RIGHT AND FAR RIGHT: *These two photos show San Francisco's Gaylord Perry in action against Atlanta on 20 August 1966 as he became the first major league pitcher to win 20 games that season. The Cy Young Award winner (1972) ended the 1966 season with a 21-8 record.*

BELOW: *Polish-born Walter Myron 'Moe' Drabowsky pitches in relief for the Orioles in the first game of the 1966 World Series with Los Angeles. The well-travelled pitcher became an unlikely hero in this game when he fanned 11 batters in his six and two-thirds innings, including six in a row in the fourth and fifth innings, to preserve Baltimore's 5-2 lead.*

was the National League MVP in 1961). In 1975 Robinson would become the first black manager in major league history.

With Matty Alou hitting for a league high of .342 and Roberto Clemente turning in his league's 1966 MVP performance, not to mention solid hitting from Willie Stargell and Don Clendenon, the Pirates began the 1966 National League pennant race as strong contenders. They were hampered by pitching weakness, however, a problem which was not shared by the Giants. Juan Marichal's 25 wins and Gaylord Perry's 21 assured them of second place.

Taking the 1966 National League pennant were the repeating Dodgers, who put together essentially the same package of skills that had gained them pennant and World Championship success the year before. Sandy Koufax, with 27 wins, and Don Drysdale, with 13, were ably assisted by Claude Osteen, Ron Perranoski and Don Sutton. Both of the Dodgers' top pitchers had held out for $100,000-plus contracts, big money in those days, although with receipts from TV broadcasts totalling $27.5 million in 1966 baseball was no stranger to big money. For Koufax, 1966 was to be his last season. Faced with painful arthritis in his left elbow which doctors warned him would render the arm useless if he pitched another season, the popular Koufax, who displayed such mastery that he was elevated to the Hall of Fame in 1971 despite his relatively brief reign of greatness, reluctantly retired and began a career as an NBC broadcaster.

With batting, baserunning and fielding from Maury Wills, Willie Davis, Lou Johnson, Jim Lefebvre and Tommy Davis backing up their pitchers, the Dodgers, who had considerably more Series experience on their side, were highly favored over the Orioles in the 1966 World Championship. As it happened, Orioles pitchers Dave McNally, Jim Palmer, Wally Bunker and Moe Drabowsky took the Dodgers in four games and kept them scoreless for the final 33 innings. This crushing defeat signalled the end of an

LEFT: *A young Nolan Ryan. Ryan pitched for the Mets from 1966 to 1971, but he didn't hit his stride until he moved to Los Angeles in 1972. In 1973, the game's greatest strikeout artist crowned the second of his seven league-leading strikeout years by getting his 383rd strikeout of the season, a new all-time major league record, on his last pitch of season.*

BOTTOM: *Sandy Koufax, the youngest player ever to be inducted into the Hall of Fame, in his new career as a sportscaster for NBC in 1968. The popular Dodgers pitching ace was forced to retire at the height of his career after a 27-9 season in 1966 when doctors informed him he would permanently lose the use of his arm if he continued throwing.*

era of sorts for the Dodgers, for in addition to the loss of Koufax through forced retirement, Maury Wills and Tommy Davis were traded over the winter, presaging a series of trades and retirements that weakened the team precipitously. Nineteen sixty-seven would see the Dodgers in eighth place.

New pitchers of promise began to attract attention. The Mets brought up a 19-year-old fastball pitcher named Nolan Ryan, the Chicago Cubs acquired hurler Ferguson Jenkins from the Phillies, and Tom Seaver, a pitcher originally signed with a $50,000 bonus to the Braves but declared a free agent because the signing took place before his college class graduated, arrived at the Mets picked out of a hat. The Milwaukee Braves moved to Atlanta in 1966, the last franchise shift in the National League to date.

With Koufax out of the picture the National League's overall batting average rose from .249 in 1966 to .256 in 1967, and Senior Circuit teams jostled for new rankings. The Cubs were contenders with Fergie Jenkins throwing the first of seven 20-win seasons, and Rookie of the Year Seaver, up to the Mets after a year of seasoning in the Mets' farm system, won his first 16 games in the majors. But in the end neither of them could stop the Cardinals, who had recently acquired Roger Maris, long unhappy with Yankee publicity since his 1961 record, and Orlando Cepeda, who celebrated his move from the Giants with 111 RBIs and a .325 average. Consistent playing by the St Louis squad led to a ten and a half game margin over San Francisco, even though a line drive off the bat of Roberto Clemente on 15 July broke Bob Gibson's right leg and kept him out of action until September.

Inspired by Carl Yastrzemski, who hit 44 home runs, 121 RBIs and averaged .326, and manager Dick Williams, who was generally credited for getting his club to play beyond itself, the Red Sox surprised everyone and clinched the American League pennant on the last day of the season after overtaking the

RIGHT: *Lou Brock of the Cardinals loses his hat as he tries to steal second against Red Sox shortstop Rico Petrocelli in the 1967 World Series. Brock still holds the all-time stolen base record of 938.*

BELOW: *Detroit Tiger Al Kaline hugs pitcher Denny McLain after the decisive run scores for the Tigers to beat the Oakland A's in the ninth inning, 14 September 1968. This gave McLain his thirtieth win that year – the first (and only) time this has been achieved since 1934.*

Twins, the Tigers and the White Sox in the final weeks. Their Cy Young Award winner Jim Lonborg had to face Bob Gibson in the Series, however, and although the Sox took the Cardinals to seven games, in the final game Gibson, who had already won the first and fourth, gave up only three hits and the Cardinals got to Lonborg for a 7-2 victory.

In the wake of the Cardinals' 1967 championship, two men long associated with the club, manager Red Schoendienst and Stan Musial, general manager since 1966, retired. The Cardinals repeated in the National League in 1968 (the San Francisco Giants came in second for the fourth consecutive year), and the Tigers ended up 12 games ahead of the pack in the American League, with special credit due to pitchers Denny McLain and Mickey Lolich, who were well supported by Al Kaline, Norm Cash, Dick McAuliffe, Jim Northrup, Willie Horton and Mickey Stanley, among others.

But 1968 will always be best remembered as 'The Year of the Pitcher' for several reasons. Detroit's McLain, the first 30-game winner since Dizzy Dean in 1934, helped his team to the pennant with a 31-6 season that earned him both the Cy Young Award and the MVP. Don Drysdale, in the twilight of his career, pitched six consecutive shutouts and set a new all-time major league record of 58 and two-thirds consecutive scoreless innings, breaking the shutout record established by Doc White in 1904 and the record of 56 consecutive scoreless innings set in 1913 by Walter Johnson. Meanwhile, Bob Gibson, who would set a new Series record by striking out 17 men in one game, won 15 of his 22 wins in a row, pitched 13 shutouts, and set a new record with an ERA of 1.12, the lowest for a pitcher with more than 300 innings in major league history, breaking Grover Cleveland Alexander's 1915 mark of 1.22 and Walter

FAR LEFT: *Billy Williams joined the Cubs in 1959 and played with them through 1974, finishing his career with the Oakland A's. His .333 average led the league in 1972. A heavy home run hitter (426 lifetime), his 2711 career hits place him in the top 50 of all time.*

LEFT: *Cuban-born Mike Cuellar was best known for his years with the Orioles, when he won at least 20 games for four of his eight seasons. But he had also played for four seasons (1965-68) with the Astros.*

BELOW: *Jim Kaat of the Twins pitching in the fifth game of the 1965 World Series. Kaat pitched in the majors from the 1950s to the 1980s, one of the longest pitching careers of all time.*

RIGHT: *As the scoreboard indicates, Cardinal Bob Gibson is about to put out the final Pirates batter in a game on 26 June 1968, thus scoring his fifth consecutive shutout. Two-time Cy Young Award winner Gibson retired with some respectable statistics – 56 career shutouts, 251 wins, and a 2.91 ERA.*

OPPOSITE BOTTOM: *Southpaw Mickey Lolich pitched for the Detroit Tigers from 1963 to 1975. His best year was 1971, when he had a 25-14 record with 308 strikeouts. In 1968, Lolich won three games against the Cardinals in the World Series to emerge as the unexpected hero.*

Johnson's 1913 mark of 1.14. Also not to be forgotten are Juan Marichal, who turned in a 26-9 season, and Tom Seaver, who won 16 games for the second year in a row. One hundred and eighty-five shutouts were pitched in the National League alone, another major league record.

Behind these displays of pitching prowess the combined batting average for both leagues sank to a record low of .236. Carl Yastrzemski captured the American League batting title with the record low average for both leagues of .305; but consistent Pete Rose got 210 hits for a .335 average. At season's end Willie Mays's home run total was 587, placing him second behind Babe Ruth; Mickey Mantle, picking up 18, moved into third place with a total of 536.

The 1968 Series was generally regarded as a duel between Gibson and McLain, but while Gibson set Series records of 17 strikeouts in one game and seven consecutive Series victories, McLain had trouble controlling the ball and dropped two games out of three. Teammate Mickey Lolich surprised everybody – including himself – with his Series performance. In the seventh game he faced Gibson in a match that went scoreless until the seventh inning, when Gibson gave up two singles and the usually dependable Curt Flood let a ball hit by Jim Northrup get by him. Two runs up, the Tigers went on to take the game, 4-1, and the Series.

Worried that such masterful pitching was slowing down the game and losing fans, who presumably preferred lots of hits and home runs, the rules committee of organized baseball approved two rules to go into effect in 1969. The pitching mound was lowered from 15 to 10 inches, and the strike zone was reduced from shoulder-to-knee to armpit-to-top-of-knee. The changes were designed to benefit hitters, and the number of .300 hitters nearly tripled, but 15 pitchers won 20 or more games in 1969, the greatest number to do so in 40 years. On 15 September 1969 Steve Carlton became the first man to strike out 19 men in

one game, a game he also lost, 4-3, to the Mets.

The 1960s closed as they had begun – with expansion. For the 1969 season the National League added the San Diego Padres and the Montreal Expos, the first major league franchise located outside the United States; and the American League added the Seattle Pilots and the Kansas City Royals (the Kansas City Athletics had moved to Oakland the year before). Each 12-team league divided itself into an Eastern and a Western Division, with the league championship to be determined for each league in a best-of-five playoff. Critics initially contended that the divisions amounted to four major leagues, but in fact the new teams and fans soon adopted appropriate league loyalties.

LEFT: Three-time Cy Young Award winner Steve Carlton, here pitching for the Cardinals (1965-71) before moving to the Phillies, was voted the best pitcher active in the majors by his fellow major leaguers in 1983. He ranks second in all-time strikeouts.

TOP LEFT: *Righthander Dave Giusti played for the Astros from 1962 to 1969, turning up as a relief pitcher for the Pirates in 1970. In 1971 his 30 saves helped the Pirates go all the way and take the World Series.*

ABOVE: *The young Luis Tiant pitched for the Indians from 1964 to 1969, moving to Boston in 1971. Perhaps his best year was 1968, when he had a 21-9 record and a spectacular 1.60 ERA.*

LEFT: *Denny McLain of the Detroit Tigers pitched the opening game of the 1968 World Series in St Louis. McLain lost the opener but won the sixth game. In 1968 McLain had his best year – a 31-6 record, .838 win percentage and 280 strikeouts.*

LEFT: *Ralph Terry, here working out at the Yankees spring training camp in Fort Lauderdale, Florida, led the league in wins (23) in 1962 and won two World Series games for their championship.*

BOTTOM LEFT: *Curt Flood of the Cardinals snags one at Fenway Park, Boston, in the sixth game of the 1967 World Series. When the Cardinals traded Flood to the Pirates after 1969, he initiated the first legal challenge to the reserve clause.*

BELOW: *Pitcher Jim Bunning began with Detroit (1955-63), went to the Phillies (1964-67), to the Pirates (1968-69) and then returned to the Phillies to end his career with a 224-184 record. He pitched three consecutive 19-win seasons for the Phillies.*

RIGHT: *Phil Niekro, the famed knuckleballer, was pitching for the Braves in Milwaukee from 1964, then followed them to Atlanta. Niekro joined the Yankees in 1984, winning his 300th game at the end of 1985; since it was a shutout and Niekro was 46, he became the oldest pitcher to attain both these feats.*

FAR RIGHT: *Jerry Koosman pitched for the Mets for 12 of his 18 years with the majors. Here he enjoys his victory in the fifth game, his second in the 1969 World Series against the favored Orioles. Koosman's best year was 1976, when he had a 21-10 record.*

Concern over how the new expansion teams would stack up against the older franchises was ironically stifled when the Mets, long held up as the example of a sub-par expansion team, somewhat inexplicably became the Miracle Mets of 1969 – the first true expansion team to take a World Championship. This they did with a team batting average that ranked them eighth in the league; eight other clubs in the league also outscored the predominantly youthful club, which was now under the management of former Dodgers star Gil Hodges.

Although Seaver's 25-7 season was excellent and Jerry Koosman's 17-9 was fine, the Mets' pitching staff was not exceptional, and as late as 13 August the Mets trailed the powerful Chicago Cubs by nine and a half games. But the Mets won 38 of their last 49 games while the Cubs collapsed, taking first place in the Eastern Division. They were picked to go down against the Atlanta Braves – Hank Aaron had hit 44 homers and Phil Niekro had 23 wins during the regular season – but instead the Mets swept the playoffs and earned the right to face an Orioles team that was considered even more unbeatable.

Baltimore's Mike Cuellar, who tied Detroit's Denny McLain for the 1969 Cy Young Award, shut down the Mets in the first game, 4-1. But the Mets won the remaining four Series contests with someone on the squad getting a hit or making an exceptional play at just the right moment, as had been the case during the regular season. In the third game Mets center fielder Tommy Agee hit a home run in the first inning, then made two plays saving a total of six runs that rank among the most sensational in World Series history.

The Mets' amazing victory became bound up in the collective American mentality with another astonishing event of the summer of 1969 – the landing of the first men on the moon. Meanwhile, at least in part due to expansion, the National League set a new attendance record of 15,094,946. With attractions like Henry Aaron in Atlanta hitting 44 home runs, Reggie Jackson of Oakland hitting 47 and Frank Howard of Washington hitting 48, the American League did not fare badly either. Expansion was, after all, only possible for a growing business. At the close of the 1960s baseball was alive and well and healthy enough to enter a decade of change unlike any it had ever faced before.

BELOW: *Nolan Ryan (30), the relief pitcher in the Mets' 5-0 victory over the Orioles in the third game of the 1969 World Series, is congratulated by Ed Kranepool (17) while Tom Seaver exults behind them.*

OPPOSITE BOTTOM: *In the 1969 World Series, Baltimore pitcher Dave McNally helped his own cause with this two-run homer, but the Orioles could not stop the 'Miracle Mets' that year. McNally, with the Orioles from 1962 to 1974, had helped them take the 1966 Series with a shutout against the Dodgers.*

CHAPTER SEVEN
The Revolutionary Decade

By any measure the 1970s stand out as one of the most revolutionary decades in the history of baseball. During these 10 years the American League would expand to 14 teams and adopt the designated hitter, and such seemingly inviolable records as lifetime home runs, career RBIs, career and season stolen bases, season strikeouts and games pitched would all be wiped out. But above all, the 1970s were to be for baseball what the 1960s had been for American society as a whole, a time when authority and tradition were challenged and new standards set. The 1970s witnessed the introduction of fancier uniforms, sideburns and beards, and of course still more new teams; they also saw the end of the players' reserve clause, long considered the cornerstone of organized baseball. Despite dire predictions from the owners that the end of the reserve clause would mean the end of baseball, its demise instead restructured the way players, owners and fans interacted with each other in ways no one could have predicted. Baseball's popularity and profitability continued to grow, but the game would never be the same.

An indication of the changes to come occurred early in 1969 when the Major League Baseball Players' Association, then three years old, boycotted spring training over a dispute involving the pension fund. As many as 125 players, including many top stars – the largest player meeting in history – met that February in New York and pledged not to sign contracts or report for spring training until the dispute was settled. The matter fell squarely in the lap of new commissioner Bowie Kuhn, who had succeeded General William B Eckert only a few weeks before. Through his intervention an agreement was reached on 25 February that compelled owners to increase their contributions to the pension fund and gave the players several across-the-board benefits, in particular relaxing eligibility requirements for the pension

A similar arrangement between Hollywood studios and their actors had been shot down by the courts as unconstitutional some years before. The owners maintained that the reserve clause was necessary to prevent wealthy clubs from buying up all the best players and destroying the competitive balance that made baseball a success.

Citing baseball's exemption from antitrust laws, the New York City District Court dismissed Flood's $3 million suit, a decision upheld by the US Circuit Court of Appeals on 7 April 1971. On 19 June 1971 the US Supreme Court, in a split decision, also ruled that the reserve clause was binding due to baseball's peculiar exemption from antitrust laws (the result of a 1922 Supreme Court decision); but at the same time the court called the exemption an 'aberration' and suggested that Congress readdress itself to the issue, particularly because all professional sports in America, with the exception of baseball, are subject to antitrust legislation.

Although Flood's case was lost, the handwriting was on the wall; the end of the reserve clause and the new era of free agency were only a few years away. In 1973 the owners agreed that players with 10 years of experience could under certain circumstances refuse to be traded; just before Christmas 1975 arbitrator Peter M Seitz ruled in the case of pitchers Andy Messersmith and Dave McNally that a player who performed for one season without a signed contract was a free agent.

Further amendments of the reserve clause followed, until in 1976, 24 players became free agents; in 1977 the number jumped to 89 and salaries began to soar. The rest is history. Far from destroying baseball, free agency has thus far proven that baseball is not an easy game to predict: from 1982-84, for instance, 12 different teams reached their league

OPPOSITE: Curt Flood swings away in a game against the Phillies in 1969. In 1970, Flood would unsuccessfully challenge the reserve clause, but his suit opened the door to other actions by players which would eventually bring about the era of free agency.

LEFT: Curt Flood (left) is accompanied by Allan Zerman, an attorney, on their arrival in New York in January 1970. Flood is on the first leg of a trip to challenge baseball's reserve clause that will eventually lead to the US Supreme Court. Flood, who played center field for the St Louis Cardinals for 12 years, was traded to the Philadelphia Phillies after the 1969 season.

BOTTOM: Charles Finley (on right), colorful owner of the Oakland A's, with his attorney John Gahrino in 1974. Finley built a powerhouse team that won three consecutive world championships. One of the more adamant opponents of free agency, Finley began to dismantle his team the following year rather than pay his stars higher salaries on the open market.

fund. The union's victory encouraged players to consider their place in the game from a more confident perspective.

On 16 January 1970 Curt Flood, a respected outfielder who had just finished his twelfth year with St Louis, filed a suit against the reserve clause. One of the better players in the majors, Flood had been paid $90,000 for the 1969 season, one of the highest salaries in either league; he objected to being traded by the Cardinals to the Phillies, asserting that the reserve clause, which traditionally sanctioned this sort of deal regardless of a player's wishes, amounted to 'a contract for perpetual service,' and he refused to be treated as 'property . . . a chattel . . . a slave for a team against his will.'

The so-called reserve clause which Flood challenged with the full support of the Major League Baseball Players' Association was in fact an accumulation of clauses and terms included in virtually every baseball player's contract for nearly a century. In one way or another it legally bound each player to his contracting team until he was sold or traded to another team, which then retained total control of the player. Unless a team consented to release a player, which as a practical matter was only done when a player was no longer of any use or had become a headache, his choice was to stay with his team or get out of baseball.

championship series. The free agent market has also kept baseball in the public eye during the off-season, as clubs vie for players. All other considerations aside, baseball has definitely seen an extraordinary growth in popularity and revenue since the establishment of free agency.

On the playing field, however, 1970 was a season of few surprises. Despite a performance from Tom Seaver that saw him strike out 19 men in one game, including the last 10 in a row for a new record, the Mets were unable to repeat a miracle and finished third in the National League's Eastern Division, one game behind the Cubs and six behind the Pirates. Four .300 hitters – Tony Perez, Pete Rose, Bobby Tolan and Bernie Carbo – combined with the solid hitting and superb defensive play of 1970 MVP Johnny Bench to propel the Reds to the top of the Western Division. The Big Red Machine then rolled over the Pirates in the playoffs and prepared for a Series against the Orioles.

The American League season was in fact a mirror of the 1969 season, with the Orioles taking the Eastern Division and the Twins taking the Western, then the Orioles again sweeping the Twins in the playoffs. Having lost to the Mets the previous year, the Orioles were picked to lose against the strong Cincinnati club, but Baltimore took the first three games, the fifth, and the Series.

Brooks Robinson performed so well in the Series, offensively and defensively, especially with amazing diving catches that neutralized Johnny Bench, that the Hall of Fame acquired the glove he used for permanent enshrinement. In other outstanding 1970 performances Hank Aaron and Willie Mays became the ninth and tenth major league players ever to compile 3000 hits, the Cubs' Ernie Banks became the ninth player to hit 500 home runs, and White Sox shortstop Luis Aparicio set a league record of 2219 games at his position – he would go on to set the all-time career record of 2581 at shortstop.

OPPOSITE: *Catcher Johnny Bench powered the Reds to the 1970 World Series while being named MVP in the National League. Bench would be named MVP again in 1972.*

ABOVE LEFT: *Orioles star Jim Palmer won the Cy Young Award in 1973, 1975 and 1976 and won 20 or more games eight times during the 1970s.*

ABOVE: *In 1971 Vida Blue won 24 games for the A's with a 1.82 ERA and walked away with both the Cy Young and MVP awards.*

ABOVE: *Oriole Brooks Robinson (left) rushes into the arms of winning pitcher Mike Cuellar after Baltimore clinched the 1970 World Series with a 9-3 victory over the Reds in game five. Robinson batted .318 in the Series, played spectacularly at third base and was named the Series' Most Valuable Player.*

Behind the pitching of Jim Palmer (20-9), Dave McNally (21-5), Mike Cuellar (20-9) and Pat Dobson (20-9), the Orioles repeated easily in the American League Eastern Division in 1971 and also became the second team in major league history with four 20-game winners (the 1920 White Sox had been the first). Baltimore's Frank Robinson displayed the kind of excellence that won the Orioles four flags in six years when on 26 June 1971, in a game against the Washington Senators, he hit back-to-back grand slam home runs.

In the American League Western Division the Oakland A's showed the stuff that would win them three consecutive pennants and three World Series beginning in 1972. Under the able management of Dick Williams, the somewhat unorthodox club featured 32 home runs from Reggie Jackson and 21 wins from Catfish Hunter, superb relief from Rollie Fingers, and an incredible Cy Young/MVP year from 22-year-old southpaw Vida Blue, who posted a 24-8 season with 301 strikeouts and a 1.82 ERA.

In other American League action, Denny McLain continued his fall from grace by dropping 22 games for the Senators, and Curt Flood left the same club for Spain after three weeks, unable to avoid unwanted publicity surrounding his suit challenging the reserve clause. The Washington franchise left town after the season and reappeared as the Texas Rangers; the Seattle Pilots had moved to Milwaukee after one season and played in 1971 as the Brewers.

In the National League Western Division, Cincinnati's power hitters failed to produce and the Reds failed to repeat, finishing fourth to a Giants club that did not succumb to the pressing Dodgers despite annoying health problems plaguing Willie Mays and Willie McCovey. A strong Pittsburgh team featuring Roberto Clemente (.341 average), Willie Stargell (48 home runs), Al Oliver, Dave Cash and Manny Sanguillen repeated in the Eastern Division and downed the Giants 3-1 in the playoffs. Although they entered the Series as underdogs because they lacked a strong pitching staff, the Pirates won in seven behind a four-hitter from Steve Blass in the seventh game and an overpowering display of excellence from Roberto Clemente, one of the finest all-around ballplayers of his generation, that brought him the national recognition he had for so long deserved.

The 1972 season began with the first general strike in baseball history (major league umpires had successfully struck 15 months earlier) when ballplayers of both leagues, demanding that owners contribute more to medical and pension funds, walked out during spring exhibition season and stayed out for 86 regular games. These games were not made up, causing some teams to play different numbers of games in 1972; the strike ended when the owners agreed to most of the players' demands. Curt Flood's challenge to the reserve clause had been formally quashed, but the Supreme Court's sympathetic comments and the players' successful actions made it clear what kind of a decade the 1970s was going to be.

Despite owner Charles O Finley's ability to exasperate, irritate, amuse and confuse his players and executives, the Oakland A's repeated in 1972 in the American League Western Division. The only real contest in the majors this year took place in the American League Eastern Division, where as late as Labor Day the Orioles, Red Sox, Tigers and Yankees were separated by only one game. The Tigers eventually finished first, half a game ahead of Boston, only to be downed by the A's in the playoffs.

In the National League the Pirates topped the Eastern Division for the third straight year. On the last day of the season Roberto Clemente, batting .312, became the eleventh player in major league history to log 3000 hits. His record was to stand at that number, for in a season marked by the deaths of former Dodgers Jackie Robinson and Gil Hodges, Clemente died the most tragically of all, in the crash of a chartered plane taking supplies to Nicaraguan earthquake victims on 31 December.

The Reds took the Western Division in a season distinguished by a new nickname manager Sparky Anderson picked up for pulling his pitchers so quickly that Reds pitchers logged only 25 complete games in 1972. However, Captain Hook's boys took the Pirates in a playoff that went down to the wire and in the end was settled in the bottom of the ninth in the last game by a wild pitch from the Pirates' Bob Moose. Hurling for a team that finished in the cellar, the most exciting pitching of the season came from Steve Carlton, traded from the Cardinals to the Phillies, who completed 30 of 41 starts, won 27 and lost 10, struck out 310 and posted a 1.98 ERA.

LEFT: *Athletics left fielder Joe Rudi makes an amazing game-saving catch of Denis Menke's drive in the ninth inning of the second game of the 1972 World Series. The A's won the game 2-1, and took the Series from the Reds in seven games for their first World Championship since 1930. Six of the seven games were decided by only one run.*

RIGHT: *Steve Carlton prepares to deliver a pitch to the plate for the Phillies. Nicknamed 'Lefty', Carlton once struck out 19 batters in a single game. Carlton won the Cy Young Award in 1972, 1977 and 1980.*

OPPOSITE TOP: *Roberto Clemente hit .317 while playing outfield for the Pittsburgh Pirates from 1955 to 1972. In the course of his career he won three batting titles and was named MVP in the 1971 World Series. Clemente delivered his 3000th hit on the last day of the 1972 season, and was tragically killed in an airplane crash in December of that year.*

OPPOSITE BOTTOM: *Cincinnati Reds manager Sparky Anderson has a few heated words with the umpire, while Reds catcher Johnny Bench tries to intercede.*

The World Series between the eccentric A's and the Big Red Machine was one of the strangest and closest championship contests ever. Oakland's Gene Tenace made World Series history by hitting home runs in his first two at bats, but six of the seven games in this lean Series, including the last, were decided by only one run; the A's averaged .207 as a team and the Reds averaged .208. Also memorable was an amazing catch in the second game by Oakland's Joe Rudi that kept the A's alive and demonstrated the hit-by-hit and play-by-play style that characterized an A's club that became the only team except the Yankees to win three World Series in a row, 1972-74.

Another players' strike was narrowly averted in March 1973 when the owners agreed to outside arbitration in salary negotiations (players with 10 years of experience – the last five on the same club – were also permitted to refuse trades). But the big news at the beginning of the 1973 season concerned one of the most revolutionary rule changes in the history of the modern game: the adoption by the American League, on a three-year trial basis, of the designated hitter. The National League refused to try the DH even on this basis, but the American League was so happy with the results that it adopted the DH permanently at the end of the 1973 season. It clearly had the desired effect of raising the overall batting average and scoring more runs in an American League season that set new attendance records. And contrary to fears that the DH would put an end to pitching records, 1973 turned out to be a year of the pitcher for

the American League, with 12 pitchers winning 20 or more games, including five no-hitters. Two no-hitters were pitched by Nolan Ryan, recently arrived from the Mets to the Angels, who also pitched two one-hitters and set the new all-time season strikeout record of 383, one better than Sandy Koufax's 382, on his final pitch of the season. So far the National League has agreed to use the DH in World Series games played in the American League's home park.

The Oakland A's topped the American League Western Division for the third straight year in a season that featured 32 home runs and 117 RBIs from MVP Reggie Jackson and 20-win seasons from Catfish Hunter, Vida Blue and Ken Holtzman. Excellent pitching from Jim Palmer, Mike Cuellar and Dave McNally returned the Orioles to the top spot in the Eastern Division, but Oakland took the pennant in the playoffs in five games.

In the National League, 1973 was almost a rerun of the Mets' miraculous 1969 season. On 30 August they were in last place in the Eastern Division, but fired by relief pitcher Tug McGraw's 'Ya gotta believe!' they won 20 of their last 28 games and took the division title on the last day of the season. In the playoffs with Western Division champs the Cincinnati Reds, who had come from 11 games behind the Dodgers to top them by three and a half games, the Mets won in five behind excellent pitching from Tom Seaver, Jerry Koosman and John Matlack. Many will recall the free-for-all in the third game between Pete Rose and Bud Harrelson.

BELOW: *Oakland's free-swinging Reggie Jackson takes another hard cut at the ball during the 1973 World Series against the New York Mets. In his eight years with the A's (1968-75), Jackson led the league in homers twice, runs scored twice, and RBIs once. Jackson won the Most Valuable Player award in 1973.*

LEFT: *Tug McGraw, star reliever for the New York Mets, delivers during the 1973 season. McGraw's enthusiasm and excellent pitching helped the Mets to win 20 out of their last 28 games to clinch the Eastern Division on the last day of the season.*

BELOW: *Ken Holtzman's shutout in game two of the 1974 American League divisional playoffs helped the A's take the pennant. His home run in game four of the World Series helped the A's take it all.*

But the Mets' dream of repeating their 1969 miracle crumbled in the Series. After leading the A's three games to two, they lost in seven. Oakland manager Dick Williams, despite two consecutive Series wins, found himself unable to tolerate owner Finley's interference and resigned. Much of the excitement of the 1973 Series, however, was overshadowed by Hank Aaron's assault on Babe Ruth's career record of 714 home runs. 'The Hammer' hit 40 home runs that year, bringing his career total to 713 (teammates Darrell Evans hit 41 and Dave Johnson hit 43, making the Braves the first major league club to boast three 40-home-run men in a season). There was no longer any doubt that Ruth's record would fall in 1974.

When the spotlight came up on the 1974 season, it inevitably was fixed right where it had been at the end of the 1973 season: on Hank Aaron's bid for glory. As it happened, the Atlanta Braves opened in Cincinnati, and since the team management and the fans not unnaturally hoped to have Aaron 'deliver' before the home crowd, there was talk that Aaron might sit out those games at Cincinnati. However, Commissioner Kuhn ruled that Aaron had to play – and sure enough, he hit his 714th home run on opening day, thus tying Ruth's record. But on 8 April, back in Atlanta for the opening game there, Aaron obliged by hitting the 715th and record-breaking home run. Aaron would go on hitting homers until he retired in 1976 with a career total of 755, a number that now seems as secure as Babe Ruth's 714 once seemed.

After that, the 1974 season was bound to seem a bit of an anticlimax. In the National League Western Division, the Dodgers moved into first place during the first week and never gave it up, although the Reds were only four games behind at the end. In the Eastern Division, the Pirates barely nosed out the Cardinals by one and a half games, but then their heavy hitters such as Richie Hebner, Willie Stargell and Al Oliver were held down by the Dodgers' pitching (Don Sutton gave up only seven hits in winning two games) and the Dodgers took the pennant.

In the American League Eastern Division, the Orioles repeated, but only by winning 27 of their final 33 games. In the Western Division, the flamboyant Oakland A's also repeated, although at times it seemed that their main opponent was their owner, Charles O Finley. In the playoffs, the A's went on to defeat the Orioles in four games behind the superb pitching of Catfish Hunter, Vida Blue, Ken Holtzman and Rollie Fingers.

In the World Series, it was the veteran Dodgers against the upstart A's, and the new kids on the block took it, four games to one – although it was no pushover, as four of those games were decided by 3-2 scores, and the A's relied on their ace reliever, Rollie Fingers, in all four of their victories. One Dodger who would never forget the 1974 season was reliever Mike Marshall, who had appeared in 106 games, an all-time major league record. And Lou Brock of the Cardinals broke Maury Wills's 1962 record of 104 stolen bases in a season – Brock stole 118 to add to what would eventually be the major league record (938) for a career of stolen bases.

OPPOSITE TOP: Henry Aaron sets himself at the plate prior to his 714th home run that will tie Babe Ruth's record.

OPPOSITE BOTTOM LEFT: Hammerin' Hank is greeted at the plate by his teammates on 8 April 1974 following his record-breaking 715th home run in Atlanta.

OPPOSITE BOTTOM RIGHT: The new home run king is embraced by his mother following his historic shot. Aaron would go on to establish lifetime records of 755 home runs and 2297 RBIs.

LEFT: Lou Brock at the plate for the St Louis Cardinals. Brock broke Maury Wills' single-season stolen base record in 1974 by swiping 118 bases. Brock would lead the National League in stolen bases eight times.

The 1975 season would go down in the history of baseball as the turning point for two major 'routes' that organized baseball had been following. One of these came at the beginning of the season, when Frank Robinson became the first black manager in the major leagues. Robinson managed the Cleveland Indians through 1975 and had his contract renewed for 1976. It would be some years, though, before it became clear that Frank Robinson had not exactly opened up the management ranks for blacks the way Jackie Robinson had done for players.

Meanwhile, on the field during the 1975 season, in the National League Western Division the Dodgers had no chance to repeat against a Cincinnati Reds team that won 108 games. In the Eastern Division, the Pirates repeated, but then lost to the Reds in the playoffs in three straight games.

In the American League Western Division, the reigning World Champions, the A's, repeated. But the biggest surprise of the season came in the Eastern Division, where the Red Sox – powered by Carl Yastrzemski, Dwight Evans, Carlton Fisk, Jim Rice and Fred Lynn – ended up in first place. To top that, the Red Sox went on to beat the A's in the playoffs. Even then, the Red Sox were regarded as pushovers for the Big Red Machine. Instead, the Bosox extended Cincinnati to a seventh game, and not until Joe Morgan's single drove in the winning run in the game's ninth inning did the Reds take the World Series. Everyone agreed that it was one of those Series where the losers had brought as much glory to the game as did the winners.

OPPOSITE: *Right fielder Dwight Evans hits a liner through the gap. 'Dewey,' who joined the Red Sox in 1972, became a perennial Golden Glover.*

LEFT: *After joining the Red Sox in 1972, Carlton 'Pudge' Fisk was named Rookie of the Year and continued to backstop the team throughout the rest of the decade. Perhaps his most memorable hit was the twelfth-inning, game-winning home run that sent the 1975 World Series to a seventh game.*

BOTTOM LEFT: *BoSox slugger Jim Rice succeeded Carl Yastrzemski in left field, and later, as team captain. Rice won the league MVP award in 1978 only to see the Sox lose a one-game divisional playoff to the Yankees.*

BOTTOM RIGHT: *Carl Yastrzemski delivers another blow for the Red Sox. During his 23-year career for the team, Yaz broke both the 400-homer and 3000-hit barriers, the first American League player ever to do so. Yaz's dream of a World Championship, however, was never realized.*

But even this action was upstaged by the second turning point of 1975, when on 23 December Peter Seitz, an otherwise unknown arbitrator, issued a momentous decision. Two players, Andy Messersmith and Dave McNally, had played during the 1975 season under 'renewed contracts' and thus claimed they were now 'free agents.' The arbitrator ruled in the players' favor, thus effectively eliminating the reserve system that had been at the very heart of organized baseball for almost a century. But the players were willing to accept that an absolutely unrestricted system of free agents would threaten organized baseball, so they agreed to negotiate a compromise.

When the 1976 season was due to start, the issue of free agents was still unresolved, but both players and owners agreed to continue the negotiations. It was not until 12 July, the day before the All-Star game, that a compromise was announced. After five years, a major league player could ask to be traded (and could veto up to six clubs); if he was not traded,

he became a free agent; after six years in the majors, a player automatically became a free agent and could negotiate with up to 13 clubs participating in that year's draft. Many people predicted that this was going to be the ruination of the major leagues because all the good players would soon be bought up by a few rich clubs. In fact, it did not work out that way over the long run, although there was no denying that, with the reserve clause breached, the way was open to steadily increasing salaries.

During 1976 it did seem as though big money might make the difference. George Steinbrenner had bought up some expensive talent such as Catfish Hunter and Ken Holtzman, and with Billy Martin managing, the Yankees went on to take first place in the American League Eastern Division. In the Western Division, the Kansas City Royals, led by George Brett's league-winning .333 batting average, beat out the Oakland A's. In the playoffs, the Yankees won, but only by taking the fifth and deciding game on Chris Chambliss's ninth-inning homer.

LEFT: *In a test of baseball's reserve clause, Dave McNally hurled the 1975 season for the Montreal Expos after many successful seasons with the Baltimore Orioles. He finished his career with 184 wins and a lifetime 3.24 ERA.*

BOTTOM: *Pitcher Andy Messersmith was one of the first two free agents. In 1975 Messersmith tossed seven shutouts while playing without a contract.*

137

RIGHT: *George Brett sets himself at his third base position. After joining the Royals in 1974, Brett quickly established himself as a team leader, winning batting titles in 1976 and 1980 (an MVP year).*

BELOW: *Combative Yankees manager Billy Martin has one of his many turbulent altercations with umpires. This one was during the 1976 World Series against the Reds.*

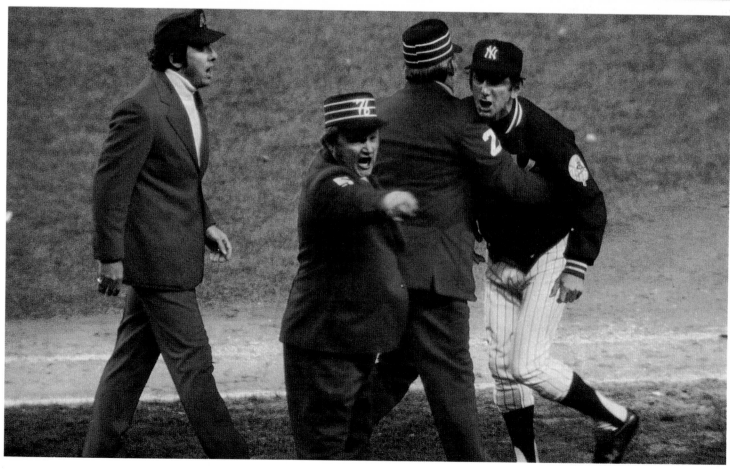

In the National League, the Phillies beat out the Pirates in the Eastern Division while the Reds defeated the Dodgers again for the Western Division title. Then the Reds, with five players hitting over .300 and a team average of .280, beat the Phillies in three straight games. In the World Series, the Reds continued their winning ways, defeating the Yankees in four straight games. So for all the talk about Fat Cats playing fast and loose with baseball players, it seemed as though the old traditions still held their own: the Reds, after all, were the first professional baseball team.

But beyond the publicity about free agents and high salaries, there was no denying that the character of baseball had been undergoing some crucial changes. The expansion in the number of teams plus the prominence of television – both in terms of the money it now provided and the exposure it gave to a broad public – combined to exert a strong influence on many aspects of the 'national pastime.' The minor leagues, for instance, had been gradually pushed into the shadows by the intense interest generated by the major league teams. Meanwhile, on their other flank the minor leagues were under pressure from college teams as a source of new players.

To some degree, the emergence of college teams as spawning grounds for major league players was a revival of an old tradition. In the early years of the century, many major leaguers used to come over from college teams – Christy Mathewson and Lou Gehrig are only two of the more exceptional models. But then college baseball went into eclipse, and many a college that would generate thousands of fans (and dollars) for its football games would hardly know its baseball team existed. But now, by the late 1970s, college teams were coming back into prominence. Because of the climate, which allows for longer seasons, the

LEFT: *Cincinnati's Johnny Bench rounds the bases. Bench caught for the Reds from 1967 to 1983 and helped power the Big Red Machine to the World Championship in 1975 and 1976.*

BOTTOM: *Jim 'Catfish' Hunter became a free agent at the end of the 1974 season and signed a $3 million-plus contract with the Yankees. Here Hunter pitches in his first victory for the Yankees during the 1975 season on his way to 23 wins.*

ABOVE: *University of Texas coach Cliff Gustafson, the winningest coach in collegiate baseball, gets a ride from his players following a 4-3 College World Series victory over Alabama for the 1983 National Championship.*

RIGHT: *Yankees catcher Thurman Munson tags out Dodger Steve Garvey during the opening game of the 1977 World Series.*

southern and southwestern states such as Arizona, Texas, Florida, and California tended to be producing the more dominant teams, but even such schools as the University of Maine were fielding teams to be reckoned with. Inevitably, there was a down side to this phenomenon: Some students of the game feel that the college stars are rushed into the majors too quickly, that there is still no substitute for the minors' 'school of hard knocks.' But it does appear that college baseball is gaining a new following.

As evidence that major league baseball was trying to respond to the new dynamics of its public, the American League in 1977 chose to add two new teams, the Toronto Blue Jays and the Seattle Mariners. Naturally, it would be some time before such expansion teams could become serious contenders for postseason play, but in the American League Western Division the Kansas City Royals repeated in first place by defeating the Texas

Rangers, neither team having existed before 1969. Much of the commotion of the 1977 season was provided by the American League Eastern Division, particularly by the Yankees with their quarrelsome trio: owner George Steinbrenner, manager Billy Martin and superstar Reggie Jackson. Yet somehow the Yankees came through, winning 38 of their last 51 games to beat out the Orioles and the Red Sox (the latter team with a total of 213 home runs, the fourth highest total in league history).

In the National League Eastern Division, the Phillies came out on top again, with the Pirates in second place. In the Western Division, the Dodgers turned the tables on the Reds, beating them by the same 10 games the Dodgers had lost by in 1976. The Dodgers were now being managed by Tommy Lasorda, who had replaced Walt Alston after his 23 years managing the team. In the National League playoffs, the Phillies looked mighty strong, what with

LEFT: *Mike Schmidt has been a fixture at third base for the Philadelphia Phillies since breaking into baseball in 1972. Known for belting the long ball, Schmidt has led the National League in homers eight times and picked up back-to-back Most Valuable Player awards in 1980 and 1981. Schmidt hit .381 during the Phillies' 1980 World Series victory.*

TOP LEFT: *Reggie Jackson being congratulated by a teammate following a home run. 'Mr October' belted five home runs, including three on three consecutive pitches, during the Yankees' 1977 World Series victory over the Dodgers.*

TOP RIGHT: *Fleet Ken Griffey patrolled the outfield for the Cincinnati Reds and hit better than .300 in each of their world championship seasons (1975-76).*

BOTTOM LEFT: *Rod Carew on deck. Voted Rookie of the Year in 1967, he went on to capture seven batting titles in his 12 years with the Minnesota Twins. Carew joined the Angels in 1979.*

BOTTOM RIGHT: *Rusty Staub at the plate for the Detroit Tigers. Staub played for many teams during his 23-year career, hitting 292 home runs.*

OPPOSITE: *Steve Garvey began playing first base for the Dodgers in 1969 and proved to be one of the National League's most consistent and productive hitters during the 1970s. Garvey was named the league's Most Valuable Player in 1974 and later set a league mark of 1207 consecutive games played.*

veteran Steve Carlton's 23-10 record, Mike Schmidt's 40 homers and Greg Luzinski's 39 homers, but the Dodgers took the pennant. In the American League playoffs, the Yankees met the Royals; they went the full five games, with the Yankees taking the pennant by coming up with three runs in the ninth inning of the final game.

So once again, it was World Series time, and in what seemed like one of baseball's eternal rivalries, the Yankees were playing the Dodgers. The Dodgers boasted four 30-home-run hitters – Steve Garvey, Reggie Smith, Ron Cey and Dusty Baker – but iron-

ically, Yankee home runs beat them: particularly memorable were 'Mr October' Reggie Jackson's five, including three consecutive homers on three consecutive pitches. Jackson also scored 10 runs, four of them in a single game. The Yankees ended up winning the World Series, four games to two.

During the regular season, Rod Carew won his sixth American League batting title with his .388 average (the best since Ted Williams's .388 in 1957) and his 239 hits, while Lou Brock broke another of those landmark records, Ty Cobb's career total of 892 stolen bases, and was now in the clear for the all-

BELOW: *Dodgers manager Tommy Lasorda talks with first baseman Steve Garvey in the LA dugout. Since taking over as manager in 1976, Lasorda has won six Western Division championships, four pennants, and two World Series titles.*

BOTTOM: *Ron Guidry pitches for the Yankees. In 1978, 'Louisiana Lightning' posted a 25-3 record and a 1.74 ERA on his way to the Cy Young Award. His .893 winning percentage set a record for a 20-plus game winner.*

time major league record of 938 stolen bases.,

On the surface, the outcome of the 1978 season seemed predictable: all four teams from 1977 repeated as division winners. Beneath the surface, however, there were some twists and turmoil. In the National League Eastern Division, the Phillies beat out the Pirates again, while in the Western Division the Dodgers beat out the Reds by winning 22 of their last 37 games. In the playoffs, the Dodgers beat the Phillies for the second year in a row.

In the American League, the Kansas City Royals won the Western Division for the third year in a row.

ABOVE: *Lou Brock of the St Louis Cardinals breaks for second base in an attempted steal against the Pirates. In 1977 Brock broke Ty Cobb's long-standing stolen base record of 892, on his way to achieving the all-time mark of 938.*

But once again, most of the season's fireworks were generated by the American League Eastern Division. The Yankees were feuding again, climaxing with Steinbrenner's firing of Billy Martin after Martin made a public crack referring to Steinbrenner having been charged with illegal campaign contributions. When Bob Lemon took over as manager in late July, the Yankees were ten and a half games out of first place, yet on literally the last day of the season, they pulled up to a tie with the Red Sox, who had collapsed during September. In the one-game playoff, the Yankees proved to be too much for the Sox, and with Ron Guidry pitching, Bucky Dent's three-run homer, and Reggie Jackson's game-winning homer, the Yankees took the division title. Now the Yankees were on a roll, and they beat the Royals three games to one to take the American League pennant.

The World Series thus became a rerun of 1977. When the Yankees lost the first two games, some fans at least probably felt they were about to get their comeuppance. Instead, their heavy hitters – Reggie Jackson, Bucky Dent, Lou Piniella, and Thurman Munson – got hot, Graig Nettles contributed some extraordinary fielding, and the Yankees went on to take the next four games and the World Series. To those who had been predicting that the open bidding for free agents plus the Yankees' big treasury were about to start another unstoppable dynasty, the signs were clear: two straight Yankee championships. In fact, for at least another 20 years neither the Yankees nor any other team would be able to repeat as World Champions, further proof that baseball remained a sport of unpredictables.

OPPOSITE LEFT: *Catcher Thurman Munson played for the Yankees from 1969 to 1979. Voted Rookie of the Year in 1970, Munson helped to lead the team to three pennants, hitting .373 in three World Series.*

OPPOSITE RIGHT: *Yankees fire-balling reliever Goose Gossage tries to shut down the opposition. Gossage was the main stopper on the Yankee staff from 1978 to 1983.*

ABOVE: *Graig Nettles leaps for a low line drive from his position at third base. He was a defensive force for the Yankees from 1973 to 1983, but also was a threat at the plate, hitting 27 homers in 1978 and batting .333 in the playoffs.*

LEFT: *Alan Trammell joined the Detroit Tigers in 1977 and has sparkled at shortstop ever since. He helped lead his team to a World Series victory in 1984.*

RIGHT: *George Foster broke into baseball in 1969 with the Giants, and then moved on to star with the Reds and the New York Mets. While at Cincinnati he was the league's home run king in 1977-78 and was named the Most Valuable Player in 1977.*

BOTTOM: *Don Baylor, designated hitter and outfielder for the California Angels from 1977 to 1982, powered his way to the league's MVP award in 1979. Baylor hit 36 homers, batted in 139 runs and scored 120.*

No better proof of this could be provided than by the 1979 season, for after two years of the same teams' dominance, all four divisions were won by new teams. In the American League Eastern Division, the Yankees again made the headlines, with Bob Lemon being replaced as manager in June by none other than Billy Martin (who himself would be fired in October) and catcher Thurman Munson dying in a plane crash, but this time they couldn't come through on the field. Instead, the Baltimore Orioles beat off the Brewers and the Red Sox and with 102 wins took the division title. In the Western Division, the winner was the California Angels, a team that had been finishing an average of 23 and a half games out during their first 18 seasons. Despite such stalwarts as Rod Carew, Don Baylor and Brian Downing, and the superb pitching of Nolan Ryan (223 strikeouts for the season), the Angels lost to the Orioles three games to one in the playoffs.

In the National League Eastern Division, the Pirates finally dislodged the Phillies from first place, while in the Western Division the Reds took over from the Dodgers. In the playoffs, the Pirates, riding the crest of good 'family' vibes sparked by Willie Stargell, defeated the Reds in three straight games.

LEFT: *Willie Stargell strokes a double for the Pirates during the 1979 World Series against the Orioles. In 1979 Stargell won both the league and Series MVP awards. Stargell had three home runs and four doubles against the Orioles.*

BELOW: *Eddie Murray, one of the American League's most dangerous hitters, bats against the Pirates in the 1979 World Series.*

ABOVE: *The Pittsburgh Pirates celebrate their 1979 World Series victory over the Baltimore Orioles as they lead hero Willie Stargell (second from right, top) off the field.*

The 1979 World Series was immediately dubbed a 'railroad series' because the two hometowns, Baltimore and Pittsburgh, were connected by train lines. But in the end, it was the foul weather that seemed to be a major factor: the best that could be said was that the rain and cold hit both teams equally. Baltimore came out of the first four games with a three-to-one lead, and it seemed the Pirates were doomed. But the Pirates won the last three games (as impossible as it seemed, three other teams had previously done this in Series play) and took the World Series.

Several personal records were set during the 1979 season – J R Richard of the Astros, for instance, struck out 313 hitters, a league record for righthanders, while two brothers, Phil Niekro (21-20) and Joe Niekro (21-11), led the National League in wins. But the most telling record was the total attendance during 1979 at major league games – 43,548,450 – thus breaking the record for the fourth straight year. As the 1970s came to an end, for all the confrontations and challenges, it was clear that baseball had not lost its appeal.

RIGHT: *Phil Niekro began pitching for the Braves in 1964, when they were still in Milwaukee. Niekro posted 21 wins for the Braves in 1979 on his way to 300-plus career wins.*

CHAPTER EIGHT

High and Outside: The 1980s

If the 1980s for major league baseball had to be summed up in a phrase, perhaps the most appropriate would be 'the decade of disruptions.' Just when it seemed no decade could be more unsettled than the 1970s, just when it seemed that baseball needed some years off from shenanigans, the 1980s came along as one of those periods when the game on the field was threatened with being overshadowed by the games being played off-field. Disputes over free agency and salaries, strikes and walkouts, drugs and brawls, charges of racism and collusion, 'fixed' balls and bats – these were only a few of the episodes and issues that would keep baseball and its fans in continual turmoil during the 1980s.

The first sign that the decade was not going to go smoothly began even before spring training in 1980, with the expiration on 31 December 1979 of the contract, in effect since July 1976, between the owners and players. In particular, the owners, alarmed by the large salaries they had been conceding to the free agents (thereby driving up the average salary of all major league baseball players from about $50,000 in 1976 to almost $200,000 by 1980), now decided to impose a new condition: any team that lost a free agent should be allowed to choose a player from the club that signed the free agent. The players regarded this as putting the brakes on true bidding. Attempts to negotiate over the winter failed, and the players actually walked out of their final week of spring training, but they returned to start the season – with the warning that they would go on strike on 23 May if the issue was not resolved by then. It was, but only minutes before the deadline and only partially: a committee was set up with two player reps and two general managers to study the subject of free agents, with a new deadline of 31 January 1981.

Clearly this was a stalling tactic, but it did allow the 1980 season to proceed. In the National League

Western Division, the regular season ended in a tie between the relatively young Houston Astros and the decidedly veteran Los Angeles Dodgers. The Astros won the playoff game thanks to Joe Niekro's pitching. The race in the Eastern Division was almost as close, with the Phillies locking up first place only with Mike Schmidt's homer against Montreal in their next-to-last game of the season. The Phillies then defeated the Astros, three games to two, but with four games going into extra innings, to take the pennant.

In the American League Western Division, the Kansas City Royals won handsomely, with the Oakland A's 14 games behind in second place. In the Eastern Division, the 1979 winner, the Baltimore Orioles, fought it out to the end with the 1978 winner, but the Yankees won – and then fell to the Royals in three straight games.

The Royals went into the Series with some outstanding players – George Brett had fallen short of overtaking Ted Williams's 1941 average of .406 but he ended up with the best since that, a .390, while Willie Wilson had 230 hits, 133 runs, and a .326 average. But the Phillies were loaded with talent, including the veterans Steve Carlton, Pete Rose (who left Cincinnati in 1979) and Mike Schmidt. And it was Schmidt – with his two homers, seven runs batted in and a .381 average – who led the Phillies to victory, four games to two, to take the Series.

The 1980 season was the lull before the storm, and when the 1981 season began the players were still rejecting the owners' proposed compromise over the free agents issue: namely, for each 'premium' player who left a club as a free agent ('premium' to be defined by a complicated formula based on statistics), the club would be given a replacement chosen from a list provided by the club that signed the free agent. Again, the players saw all this as effectively stifling free trade in good players, but they agreed to play until yet another deadline – 11 June 1981.

OPPOSITE: *One of the premier hitters and fielders of the American League, George Brett has played with the Kansas City Royals since 1974. Within his first three years, Brett accumulated 509 hits and took the batting title in 1976 with a .333 average. In 1980 he seemed on his way to a .400-plus average, but settled for .390. In 1985 he turned in another fine season to help the Royals take the World Series. Brett retired in 1993 after 21 seasons with Kansas City, and 3154 hits.*

LEFT: *Pete Rose, during his 'interregnum' with the Phillies, continued to give his all, as seen here in one of his patented head-first slides. Whatever Rose may have lacked in power with his bat, he more than made up for with consistent hitting and scrappy running.*

BELOW: *Steve Carlton won three Cy Young awards and holds second place in lifetime strikeouts. He was elected to the Hall of Fame in 1994.*

BOTTOM: *The Royals' Willie Wilson led the league in stolen bases (83) in 1979 and BA (.332) in 1982.*

RIGHT: *Dave Parker played with the Pirates from 1973 to 1983, then moved over to the Reds. 'The Cobra' had his best personal year in 1977, when he led the league in batting average (.338), hits (215) and doubles (44). He repeated in 1978 with a league-leading .334. His power helped the Pirates to three pennants and the World Series championship in 1979.*

BOTTOM: *Southpaw Fernando Valenzuela made his debut with the Dodgers in 1981, winning both the Cy Young Award and Rookie of the Year Award. He was an important factor in the Dodgers' World Series victory over the Yankees that year. After taking a year off from the majors in 1992, he returned with the Orioles in 1993.*

The season thus got underway in an apparently normal way, with tight races in all four divisions of the majors. In the Western Division of the National League, much of the excitement was generated by a 20-year-old southpaw rookie who spoke barely any English – Fernando Valenzuela of the Dodgers, who won his first eight games (five by shutouts) in 1981. In the American League, as 11 June approached, the Yankees and Orioles were battling it out again, while in the league's Western Division the Oakland A's were holding first place with the Texas Rangers hot on their heels.

When 11 June came and went with no agreement on the free agent issue, the players went out on strike on 12 June and stayed out, day after day for 50 days – the longest strike in the history of American professional sports. What happened to Americans as they had to cope during those long weeks without their national pastime is more the subject of sociology or psychology than a history of baseball, despite all the words written by sportswriters even when there were no games being played.

LEFT: *This Alpena, Michigan team won the Babe Ruth Baseball World Series in 1982. Babe Ruth Baseball, founded in Trenton, New Jersey in 1952, is for 13- to 15-year-olds and is one of many youth baseball leagues across the country. Some leagues stress participation and learning more than proficiency and winning, but all encourage youths of both sexes to get out and play ball.*

BELOW: *World Series Park, home of the annual Little League World Series in Williamsport, Pennsylvania. The Little League was founded in this city in north central Pennsylvania in 1939 by Carl E Stolz; it began with only three teams of boys aged 8 to 12. After World War II, Little League spread rapidly until today teams from all over the world compete through a series of playoffs to make the semifinals and finals that are held here.*

No major league games, that is. In fact, there was a lot of baseball being played throughout the country during that 50-day 'drought.' Youth baseball, for one, went on, and the minor leagues were rediscovered by many Americans during the summer of 1981. Yet the plain fact was that, for all their talented and hard-working players – many of whom, of course, continue to supply the majors – the minor leagues were no longer the force they had once been; as soon as the strike was settled, the minors slipped back into the shadows.

Seven hundred and fourteen major league games had been cancelled during the summer of 1981. It was 31 July before players and owners reached a compromise: teams that lose a 'premium' free agent can draw from a pool of players established by all clubs (not just those that sign free agents), and the teams that lose any players from this pool will be compensated from a fund maintained by all major league clubs. The point here is to distribute the impact and cost so that owners would not be afraid of bidding generously for premium free agents. It was then announced that the players would go at once into a 10-day training session before taking up official games. It was further announced that the owners had agreed to split the 1981 season: teams in first place in each division when they quit on 11 June would play the teams in first place at the end of the remainder of the season, to decide division winners. To further unsettle things, if the same team happened to win both parts, it would have to play the runner-up from the second half only, to determine the winner.

PRECEDING PAGES: *Little League baseball has come far from the days of makeshift gear and improvised uniforms; modern Little Leaguers wear sleek colorful uniforms and work with the latest equipment. By the time Little Leaguers get into the playoffs – intercity, regional, and beyond – the teams are amazingly proficient, as demonstrated by these Little Leaguers in the 1985 State Championship playoff series, held in Chrisolm, Minnesota.*

OPPOSITE TOP: *Founded in 1950 in Washington, Pennsylvania, the Pony League joined with the Colt League in 1959 to form Boys' Baseball, for 13- and 14-year-olds. This is the 1983 Santa Susana Pony All-Stars team of Simi Valley, California.*

OPPOSITE BOTTOM: *This Kirkland, Washington team represented the Western Division of the United States in the 1982 Little League World Series at Williamsport, Pennsylvania. After a series of playoffs among teams from neighboring cities, the winners have to survive state playoffs (sometimes two series, depending on population), regional playoffs, and then playoffs among teams in one of the four regions into which the country is divided. The four division winners go to Williamsport to compete against other teams from around the world.*

FAR LEFT: *Joe Niekro, who began with the Cubs in 1967 and was still pitching in 1987 (for the Indians), holds the record with Phil Niekro for most wins by brothers (520). In 1979 they shared another unusual distinction: Joe at 21-11 and Phil at 21-20 led the National League in wins.*

LEFT: *Steve Rogers joined the Montreal Expos in 1973. He retired in 1985 with a career ERA of 3.17 and 37 shutouts.*

RIGHT: *Graig Nettles played for the Yankees from 1973 to 1983 when, following a dispute with owner George Steinbrenner, he left to join the Padres. A superb third baseman who can make incredible shoestring catches, Nettles also excels at bat; he was particularly strong in 1978 when his 27 season homers and .333 average in the playoffs helped the Yankees take the World Series.*

BOTTOM SEQUENCE: *Tom Seaver, shown here during his time with the Cincinnati Reds (1977-82), began with the Mets in 1967 and ended up with them when he retired in 1987. Seaver holds several pitching records and won the Cy Young Award three times. In this sequence, he studies the batter and waits for the signal, starts his windup, continues through it, and then prepares to let loose.*

That, as it happened, did not occur, but something else that was predicted did: two teams that had the best total season records for 1981 came in second for each part and thus did not get into the division playoffs. (This was possible because the two parts of the season had unequal numbers of games.) The second part took up on 10 August in a mood of exhilaration and disorientation, and when it ended, the National League had two teams feeling mighty frustrated. The Cincinnati Reds had come in second to the Dodgers in the first part and second to the Astros in the second part; in the Eastern Division, the Cardinals were second to the Phillies in the first part, then second to the Expos in the second part. Yet the Reds and Cardinals had the most wins for the entire 1981 season. In the first round of the playoffs, though, the Dodgers beat the Astros while the Expos beat the Phillies; in the playoff finals, the Dodgers defeated the Expos to take the pennant.

In the American League Eastern Division, the Yankees had led at the end of the first part, while the Brewers won the second part; in the first round of playoffs, the Yankees beat the Brewers. In the Western Division, the Oakland A's won the first part but lost out in the second part to the Kansas City Royals; they then met in the first round of the playoffs, and the A's defeated the Royals. In the playoff finals, the Yankees beat the A's (managed by Billy Martin, no

less) three straight games, almost entirely thanks to Craig Nettles with his nine RBIs.

So it was that after all this tinkering, two of baseball's most traditional rivals came rolling into the World Series to meet for the eleventh time. The Yankees had won eight of these Series, and when the Dodgers lost the first two games in 1981, it looked like the Yankees were on their way to a ninth victory. But the Dodgers won the next four (the Yankees had done exactly the same to the Dodgers in 1978) with a true team effort, signified by the fact that Dodgers Ron Cey, Steve Yeager and Pedro Guerrero shared the MVP for the Series.

The 1981 season, for all its disruptions, saw several players attain significant records: Nolan Ryan, pitching for the Astros, got his fifth career no-hitter; Tom Seaver and Steve Carlton notched their 3000th strikeouts; and Pete Rose got his 3361st hit, thus moving ahead of Stan Musial and into a position to take on Hank Aaron's career total of 3771, second only to Ty Cobb's legendary 4191 hits.

The 1982 season was one that the Atlanta Braves will not soon be allowed to forget. They opened with a National League record of 13 straight wins; by the end of July they led the Western Division by nine games over the Padres and ten over the Dodgers. But by the end of August, the Braves had ceded first place to the Dodgers; then, on the final day of the season,

LEFT: *Dave Winfield played for San Diego from 1973 to 1980 before signing on with the Yankees for a 10-year contract worth at least $15 million. In his first four years with the Yankees, he had a total of 390 RBIs and also won three Golden Glove awards for his work in right field. In 1990 he went to the California Angels and then in 1992 to the Blue Jays, where his timely double helped them take their first World Championship. In 1993 he moved on to the Twins, ending the season with 3014 hits.*

LEFT: *Nolan Ryan, one of the all-time great pitchers, retired in 1993 holding first place in career strikeouts – 5714. In 1983 he set another all-time record with 383 strikeouts in one season. Ryan began with the Mets in 1967, went to the Angels in 1972, joined the Astros in 1980, and in 1989 went to the Texas Rangers where he ended his career. One can only speculate what he might have done with stronger teams behind him.*

BOTTOM: *Steve Howe, who pitched for the Los Angeles Dodgers from 1980 to 1983, exults in his win over the Yankees in the fourth game of the 1981 World Series. He joined the Yankees in 1991.*

the Braves took over first place, but only because the Dodgers lost to the Giants. In the league playoffs, the Braves came up against the Eastern Division's St Louis Cardinals, who had barely beat off a host of strong contenders – the Reds, Pirates, Phillies and Expos – while themselves hitting only a total of 67 home runs all season; the Braves' luck ran out as the Cardinals swept three straight to take the pennant.

Over in the American League in 1982, another of those one-in-a-thousand situations arose. In the Eastern Division, the Brewers were enjoying a three-game lead over the Orioles as they came into their final four games – as the chance of scheduling had it, against the Orioles. Incredibly, the Orioles won the first three games, so the season came down to the last game, but with the newly acquired Don Sutton on the mound, the Brewers regained first place. In the Western Division, the California Angels came out on top with no such dramatics, although they had been hard-pressed by the Royals. In the playoffs, the Angels defeated the Brewers in the first two games at Anaheim, but back in Milwaukee the Brewers took the final three and the pennant.

The 1982 World Series proved to be a hard-fought slugfest, with the teams scoring a total of 72 runs. The Brewers had some strong talents – their Robin Yount was the American League's MVP, while Pete Yukovich won the Cy Young Award. But behind the pitching of Joaquin Andujar and the superb all-round play of Darrell Porter, the Cardinals emerged from the seventh game as World Champions.

ABOVE: *Don Sutton came to the majors in 1966 with the Los Angeles Dodgers; after moving through several teams, he made headlines when he joined the Milwaukee Brewers late in 1982 and helped them win the pennant. He retired from the Dodgers and ranks fifth in career strikeouts and tenth in career shutouts.*

LEFT: *Ben Oglivie joined the Brewers' outfield in 1978 after seven years with the Red Sox and the Tigers. He led the league in 1978 with homers (41), and his 102 RBIs in 1982 helped the Brewers take the pennant.*

RIGHT: *Robin Yount, shortstop for the Milwaukee Brewers, won MVP honors in 1982 for his batting average of .331 and league-leading 210 hits, 46 doubles and .578 slugging average. That year he became the first player in history to have two four-hit games in the World Series. He retired from baseball in 1992.*

BELOW: *Rickey Henderson, then with the Oakland A's, acknowledges the response to his 119th stolen base in 1982, thus breaking Lou Brock's 1974 record of 118. Henderson stole four bases in this game and ended the 1982 season with 130, still the all-time record.*

Several individuals would also long remember the 1982 season. Rickey Henderson of the A's first broke Lou Brock's 1974 record of 118 stolen bases and ended up with 130 – one of those records that may sit there a long time. Gaylord Perry got his 300th win, only the fifteenth major league pitcher to attain this. And another who will not forget 1982 was Bowie Kuhn, the Commissioner of Baseball since 1969; some of the team owners were unhappy with his per-

formance – although how much of it was a clash of personalities and how much objective criteria would never be known – and in November enough owners voted to end his contract. They asked Kuhn to stay on, though, until a suitable successor could be found, little realizing that it would be October 1984 before his successor was in place.

But a lot would happen in major league baseball before that October. Nineteen eighty-three, for instance, was the year that drug abuse finally came out of the locker room: individual players had been in trouble for using drugs, but now four members of the Kansas City Royals alone were found guilty of using cocaine. This sparked a demand for a crackdown on the use of drugs by athletes, but just how this would be carried out was to remain an issue as Americans tried to balance their respect for individual rights against a sense that athletes should not be using drugs.

BELOW: *On 27 August 1982 Rickey Henderson set a new one-season stolen-base record with this, his 119th. Henderson led the league in stolen bases from 1980 to 1986 and 1988 to 1991, when he broke Lou Brock's career record of 938 stolen bases.*

For light relief, 1983 also produced the pine-tar bat imbroglio. On 24 July, the Yankees were playing the Royals; in the top of the ninth, George Brett hit a two-run homer to give the Royals a 5-4 lead, but Yankee manager Billy Martin rushed forward to protest that Brett's bat had more than the 18 inches of pine tar allowed. The umpire supported Martin's protest, but Lee MacPhail, president of the American League, overruled the umpire a few days later and ordered that the final part of the game be replayed. It was, some weeks later, the Yankees quickly went down to defeat, and everyone chuckled over the humor of it all.

Everyone, that is, except the Yankees, because when they played that 'funny' game against the Royals the Yankees were in hot contention for first place in the Eastern Division; somehow they lost momentum and the Orioles surged ahead, held off the Tigers, and took first place. Over in the American League Western Division, the Chicago White Sox managed to hold on to first place and so for the first time since 1959 got into postseason play, then fell to the Orioles in three straight.

In the National League Western Division, the Dodgers claimed the first place they had been done out of in 1982, while in the Eastern Division the Phillies had a fairly easy way to first place – and then went on to defeat the Dodgers in three out of four games to

the only one never to have installed lights, what was to be done now that the Cubs were clearly on the road to a World Series, where some night games were now required. After the Cubs won the first two games against the winner of the Western Division, the San Diego Padres, the debate became almost frenzied – but the Padres then resolved the problem by taking the next three games and thus the pennant.

But all this turned out to be academic, because the Tigers were not going to give up the first place they had held from day one; they defeated the Padres four games to one and became 1984's indisputable World Champions.

BELOW: Willie Hernandez joined the Cubs in 1977, went to the Phillies in 1983 and then to Detroit in 1984. That year he appeared in 80 games in relief, saved 32, won nine, and helped the Tigers to a World Series victory. Hernandez won the MVP and Cy Young awards for that year's stellar performance.

take the pennant. The Phillies were favored in the 'railroad series' against the Orioles – thanks to such future Hall-of-Famers as Mike Schmidt, Pete Rose, Joe Morgan and Steve Carlton – but the superstars failed to shine and the Orioles took the World Series, four games to one.

Along with the drug problems and the pine-tar bat, 1983 would be remembered as the season when Steve Carlton became the sixteenth pitcher to win 300 games and joined Nolan Ryan in overtaking Walter Johnson's major league career record of 3508 strikeouts. Pete Rose took over tenth place in consecutive games played with his 745, but Steve Garvey assumed first place in the National League with his 1207 consecutive games. This was also the year that Fred Lynn hit the first grand slam in the history of the All-Star game, thus helping the American League to win this fiftieth anniversary of the contest.

The 1984 season was one of those rarities where a team that won its first game, and thus could be regarded as at least sharing first place, never fell out of first place through the entire season. The Detroit Tigers rolled up a fantastic early lead, winning 35 of their first 40 games including a 17-game winning streak at one point; by 18 September the Tigers had clinched the Eastern Division title in the American League. The Royals took over in the Western Division, beating out the Twins, but then fell to the Tigers in three straight.

In the National League, the conversation piece of the year was the Chicago Cubs, who managed to hold on and win first place in the Eastern Division, thus going into postseason play for the first time since 1945. As the Cubs approached the impossible dream, the nation (or at least the sportswriters) took up a dilemma: since the Cubs' home field, Wrigley, was

RIGHT: *Bob Horner played for the Atlanta Braves from 1978 to 1986, averaging 111 hits, 73 RBIs, .278 batting and .508 slugging for nine years and hitting 215 homers. In 1987, unhappy with salary offers he received as a free agent, Horner went off to play in Japan and enjoyed great success with the fans there.*

BELOW: *Baseball was a demonstration sport in the 1984 Olympics at Los Angeles. Japan's team standing on the gold medal podium, and America's on the silver (left) indicates how well baseball is now played outside the United States.*

OPPOSITE: *Ryne Sandberg of the Cubs is knocked off his feet at second base by a charging Padres player, but Sandberg has already thrown the ball to complete the double play. Sandberg joined the Cubs in 1982 and by 1984 was already voted MVP for batting .314 and leading the league in runs (114) and triples (19). A reliable fielder and strong hitter, he retired during the 1994 season when he felt he could no longer be at his best.*

The 1984 season was also marked by the appointment of Bowie Kuhn's successor as Commissioner, Peter Ueberroth, who had presided over the immensely successful Olympic Games in Los Angeles during the summer. As it happened, baseball was introduced as a demonstration sport in those very Olympics, but the United States lost in the final to Japan's team. No one claimed this signalled the same takeover of baseball as the Japanese had managed in electronics, but it did serve as a healthy reminder that baseball has become a popular and well-played game in many countries other than the United States.

Canada and Mexico hardly need mentioning, and by now most Americans are aware that Japan supports professional teams much like those in our major leagues, although in Japan they are owned by large corporations, with stadiums, crowds and much of the paraphernalia familiar to American fans. Baseball was introduced to Japan by an American teacher back in 1873, but it long remained just an amateur sport, with college teams at the peak. Then, in the 1930s, visits by American teams and players, particularly Babe Ruth in 1934, led to the formation of professional teams after World War II (when baseball, as a matter of fact, was officially banned). Now the Japanese support two major leagues, each with six clubs that play 130-game seasons and then hold their own All-Japan Series. It is agreed that the general level of play is high; and although no Japanese player has ever enjoyed much success in the States, this is probably due more to linguistic and cultural differences than anything else. Conversely, many good American players have played for extended periods in Japan, and it is noticeable that they don't particularly demolish the Japanese: a recent case was Bob Horner, who in 1987 seemed about to clean up the opposition and long-standing records, but by the close of the season had averaged out. One of Japan's all-time stars, Sadahara Oh, recently ended his 22-year career with 868 home runs.

Japan's dedication to baseball has long since ceased to amaze Americans, and of course it is now taken for granted that baseball has strong roots in Puerto Rico, the Dominican Republic, and many other Latin American nations. (In 1985, one city in the Dominican Republic, San Pedro de Macoris, had 14 of its young men playing in the majors.) Cuba is a special case. Baseball was introduced there as early as 1878 and eventually Cuba had a team in the Triple A International League of North America. After Castro took over and the United States broke off relations with Cuba in 1961, Cuba turned to supporting two independent leagues of its own. A sure sign of its popularity is that Castro has always liked to be seen playing baseball to show that he has not lost touch with his people.

Admittedly, baseball cannot claim to be quite the international favorite that soccer has become, but it is played in more countries than most Americans might realize – England, Australia, South Africa, Netherlands, Belgium, Taiwan and Korea. Even Italy supports some semi-professional teams. Although it's

ABOVE RIGHT: *Baseball has long been used in America by politicians trying to demonstrate their 'roots' with the people. Cuban rulers do the same: Fidel Castro has always made sure he is identified with baseball, while his predecessor, Fulgencio Batista, is shown here with his staff enjoying a game in Havana.*

RIGHT: *Baseball was introduced in Cuba as early as 1878, and eventually Cuba supported numerous teams and leagues, including a team that belonged to the American-based Triple A International League. This is the Vargas Baseball Club of Cuba in pre-Castro days. Now that America has broken relations with Cuba, there are two independent leagues there.*

not likely to happen in the immediate future, perhaps the world will enjoy true peace when the Russians and Americans join together in the cry, 'Play ball!'

In the 1985 season, if ever anyone needed more proof of the way baseball had ingratiated itself with the national consciousness it was provided by the final stretch of Pete Rose's pursuit of Ty Cobb's all-time record of 4191 hits. It would be impossible to sum up all the themes and variations that permeated not only the sports pages but also editorial columns, letters to the editor, TV news and commentary, and just plain chatter as everyone speculated about what it all meant. Undoubtedly Rose helped to put the topic front and center by announcing at the outset of the season that he planned on overtaking Cobb on a particular day in August; this served to fire up speculation as to whether Rose was really as good as Cobb – whether Rose, indeed, was really that good a ballplayer. But most of this was little more than sour-graping, the same sort of resentment that Roger Maris and Hank Aaron confronted when they challenged Babe Ruth's records. In the end, Rose delivered a few weeks late, but on 11 September he got his 4192nd hit. It would have taken an unrepentant Scrooge to deny that Rose provided an emotional high for baseball fans on that occasion.

ABOVE: *Kansas City's Bret Saberhagen became an overnight sensation during his second year in the majors when he had a 20-6 record in 1985 and won the Cy Young Award. In the World Series that year, he pitched two wins for the Royals, including the seventh and deciding game. He went to the New York Mets in 1992.*

LEFT: *It was with this blow that Pete Rose, on 11 September 1985, broke Ty Cobb's career record of 4191 hits. Rose had tied the record against the Cubs at Wrigley Field; the tie-breaker was against righthander Eric Snow of the Padres. It was Rose's 13,768th at-bat, another career record he holds.*

RIGHT: *As fireworks explode over Cincinnati outside Riverfront Stadium, Pete Rose's teammates surround him at first base after his record-breaking hit.*

BELOW: *After attaining first base with his 4192nd hit, the one that broke Ty Cobb's record, Pete Rose acknowledges the cheers of the crowd at the sold-out stadium. After the celebration, Rose went right on playing.*

RIGHT: *Pittsburgh Pirate Mike Brown is tagged out at home by Phillies catcher Ozzie Virgil as he attempts to score in a game at Philadelphia's Veterans Stadium. Virgil caught for the Phillies from 1980 to 1985, but went to the Braves in 1986. He boasts a respectable .240 career average and hits his fair share of homers.*

BOTTOM: *Dwight Gooden joined the Mets in 1984, and came up with a sensational 17-9 rookie record which included 276 strikeouts and 13 games with 10 or more strikeouts. In 1985 he had 268 strikeouts and a league-leading total of 24 wins, displacing Bob Feller as the youngest pitcher ever to win 20 games. In 1988 (18-9) and 1990 (19-7) he posted good seasons, but his ongoing struggles with a drug addiction problem constantly short-circuited the great career he had promised.*

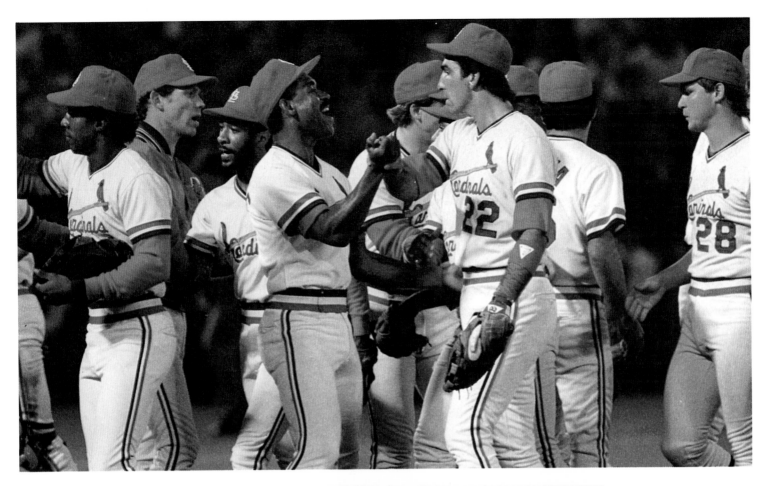

They needed one, too, after some of the low points that dogged the 1985 season, such as the trials of drug dealers in Pittsburgh that resulted in the spectacle of some major league players naming (under immunity) other players as drug-users. Then there was another strike, this time over the sharing of profits, increasingly fuelled by the astronomical fees paid by TV networks to the teams, but it collapsed after two days, and all games were made up later.

On the field, the Toronto Blue Jays gave Canada a winner when they beat out the Yankees by two games only in the American League Eastern Division. In that league's Western Division, the Royals came in ahead of the California Angels by one slim game; the Royals then fell behind the Blue Jays three games to one in the playoffs but ended up taking the pennant. In the National League, there was no great surprise when the Dodgers beat out the Padres for the Western Division. In the Eastern Division, the Mets, boosted by the sensational 24-4 record of their rookie pitcher Dwight Gooden (who displaced Bob Feller as the youngest 20-game winner in modern baseball), lost by one game to the St Louis Cardinals.

When the Cardinals beat the Dodgers for the league pennant (again, it took all seven games) there was the apparent fluke of an intrastate World Series between Missouri's Royals and Cardinals; in fact this had been surpassed by a Missouri 'intracity' Series back in 1944, when the Cardinals met the old St Louis Browns. In a rerun of their playoffs, the Royals fell behind three games to one, but then came back to take the World Series with a decisive win of 11-0 in the final game.

ABOVE: *St Louis Cardinals Ivan DeJesus (left) and Jack Clark join teammates in celebrating their defeat of the Dodgers in the 1985 National League playoffs. In the 1985 World Series, with a 3-1 game lead, the Cards were nearly ready to celebrate again when the Kansas City Royals came back to win the final three games and emerge as World Champions.*

LEFT: *Frank White of the Kansas City Royals tries to break up a double play in the 1985 World Series, but Ozzie Smith, the spectacularly agile Cardinals shortstop, has already made the throw to first.*

Along with the usual 'musical chairs' of personnel changes, the 1986 season witnessed one that says a lot about the role of baseball in American life: the just-resigned president of Yale University, A Bartlett Giamatti, took over as president of the National League. Another personnel development was not so congenial: an increasing number of free agents were realizing they were free all right – free to go nowhere, as other teams seemed unwilling to make them any offers. This led to grumbling that the owners were engaging in some sort of collusion, a concerted effort to put a lid on salaries, and the players would take the owners into arbitration on this charge.

When the season began, there was a consensus that the New York Mets would go all the way in 1986; sure enough, by 23 April they had taken over first place in the Eastern Division and they never looked back, ending up with 108 victories and a 22-game lead over the second-place Expos. In the Western

ABOVE: *Houston Astros manager Hal Lanier pours champagne over Mike Scott after he pitched a no-hitter to beat the Giants 2-0 and take the National League West title in 1986. Despite Scott's two wins in the league championship series, the Astros lost the pennant to the Mets.*

RIGHT: *Two angles on Roger Clemens, Red Sox pitching ace, as he prepares to fire one at another hapless batter. Clemens had a grand year in 1986, winning the Cy Young Award with his 24-4 record and his all-time record of 21 strikeouts in a nine-inning game. He returned in 1987 to compile a 20-9 record and collect a second Cy Young Award, and in 1990 he took his third Cy Young (21-6). In 1986 he also set the all-time record for most strikeouts in a game, with 20.*

Division, the Astros surprised everyone by beating out the favored Dodgers, the Giants, and the late-charging Reds. In the playoffs between these two 25-year-old expansion teams, the Mets were highly favored but had to go to six games to get their four wins, their chief obstacle being the Astros' ace pitcher, Mike Scott.

In the American League, the Royals and Yankees tended to be favored for their division titles but the California Angels, with the help of some oldtimers like Reggie Jackson and Don Sutton, held off the Texas Rangers and claimed the Western Division title. In the Eastern Division, a hint of what lay ahead came on 29 April when a relatively unknown Red Sox pitcher, Roger Clemens, struck out 20 Mariners in a nine-inning game, a modern major league record. Clemens then proved to be more than a flash in the pan as he went on to win his first 14 games. By 15 May, the Red Sox took over first place in their division, and despite the inevitable jokes about Boston's annual collapse, never relinquished it. The playoffs then turned out to be among the most spellbinding ever, with the Angels taking a three-to-one game lead into the fifth game and a 5-2 lead into that game's ninth inning. The Angels literally had the champagne ready to go in their locker room, but the Sox's Dave Henderson hit a two-run homer and the Sox went on to win that game, 7-6, in the eleventh inning and then take the sixth and seventh games.

ABOVE: *Houston Astros ace pitcher Mike Scott won the National League Cy Young Award in 1986.*

LEFT: *Jim Rice of the Red Sox was a durable player from 1974 to 1989, averaging 27 homers a year and three times leading the league in that category. His best year was 1978, when his 46 homers, 213 hits, 139 RBIs, and an average of .315 earned him MVP honors.*

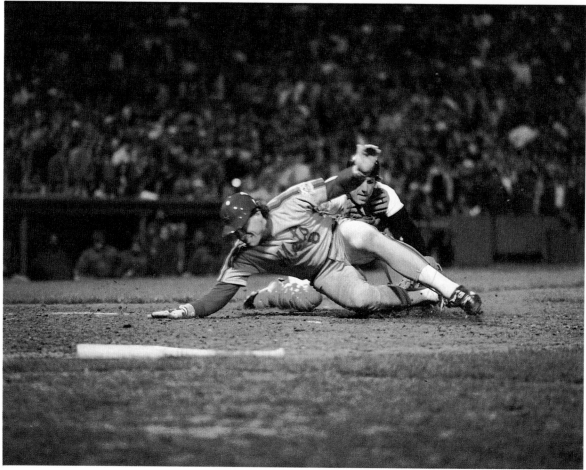

ABOVE: *In the 1986 World Series, Mets catcher Gary Carter puts the tag on a BoSox baserunner. The Mets took the Series in seven games.*

RIGHT: *Now it's Gary Carter's turn to be tagged out by Red Sox catcher Rich Gedman during the 1986 World Series.*

As the Series began, the smart words definitely favored the Mets to wipe out the Red Sox. But the Sox took the first two in Shea Stadium, and the fifth game gave them a three-to-two lead in games. But then the Red Sox did to themselves just what the Angels had done: they blew a ninth-inning lead. In the seventh game the Mets did win decisively to become World Champions, but everyone agreed that the Red Sox had done their best during 1986 for their team and all baseball fans.

The 1987 season was another of those wherein it seemed peripheral events might distract from the games on the field. Hanging over much of the season, for instance, was the question of whether the owners would be judged to have engaged in some sort of collusion in not hiring free agents. The charge under arbitration was actually in regard to 1985 free agents, but the situation was repeated in 1986 and 1987: some of the game's truly 'premium' players discovered that no teams except their current ones were offering them contracts. Different players were dealing with this in different ways: some reluctantly re-signed with their teams; some held out and then agreed to come back in May; some jumped to other teams even if it meant taking salary cuts (as did Andre Dawson and Ray Knight); some – Bob Horner at least - went off to play in Japan. It was 21 September when the arbitrator announced he had found collusion of one kind or another. What remains to be seen is just what legal force and practical impact this has; most likely the players and owners will have to negotiate their way out of this impasse.

LEFT: *Len Dykstra joined the Mets in 1985 and in only his second year in the majors found himself playing a crucial role in the Mets' pennant-winning 1986 season, batting .295, with 127 hits and 8 homers. In the World Series, Dykstra came through in the clutch again. He moved on to the Phillies in 1990 and continued to play at full throttle.*

BELOW: *Another Mets star during the 1986 World Series year was first baseman and team captain Keith Hernandez. He batted .310 for the season, with 171 hits and 13 homers, and generally kept the team moving.*

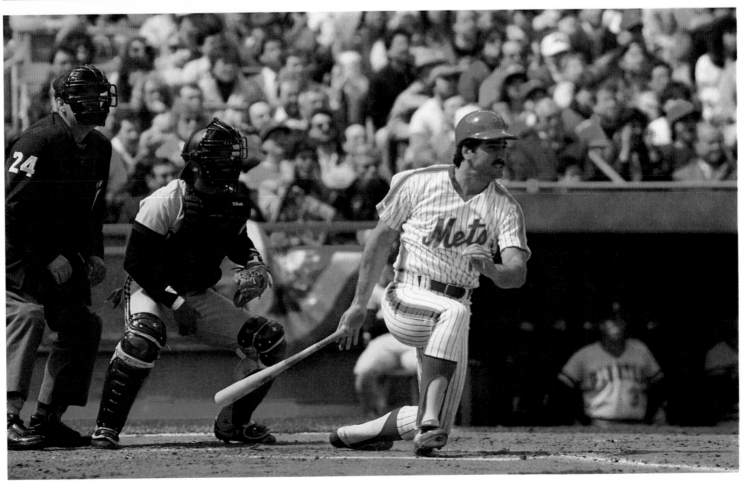

ABOVE SEQUENCE: *This four-picture sequence shows Andre Dawson in Cubs uniform taking a wicked cut at a ball, making contact, and following through – something he did often enough during his 11 years with the Montreal Expos to give him a batting average of .280 with an average of 21 homers. In 1987, angry that the Expos didn't make him a better offer, he went over to play for the Cubs; to prove that the Expos had made a mistake, he hit a league-leading 49 homers, had 137 RBIs and ended up with the MVP Award. In 1993 he went to Boston to play for the Red Sox.*

RIGHT: *Dwight Gooden pushes off from the rubber and fires one of his fearsome fastballs, the kind that earned him the name 'Doctor K.'*

LEFT: *Randy Bass played with various American teams from 1977 to 1982. In 1983, feeling his career had stalled, he went to Japan where he enjoyed success on the field and with the fans. Here he gives a 'high five' to a teammate who has hit a homer.*

RIGHT: *Mark McGwire, the Oakland A's sensational rookie of 1987, is shown touching them all on his way to a league-leading total of 49 homers (which also broke the old record for most homers for a rookie).*

FAR RIGHT: *Tony Gwynn has been an outstanding outfielder for the Padres since joining them in 1982. In 1984 he led the majors with his .351 batting average, and he did so again in 1987 with his .370 average. He led the league in 1988 with .313 and in 1989 with .336, and in 1994's inconclusive season he led the majors with a spectacular .394.*

Then there was the ongoing problem of drug use by players, thrown into the spotlight again when Dwight Gooden tested positive for cocaine in April and had to spend a month in a treatment center. For light relief, there was the case of the 'doctored' balls that occupied columns of print: because so many players seemed to be hitting so many home runs – highlighted by Mark McGwire of the A's shattering the all-time rookie record for home runs (38 by Wally Berger in 1930 and Frank Robinson in 1956) with an amazing grand total of 49 – everyone began to speculate whether the balls were being made differently. Scientific tests seemed to show that this was not so, but many an old pro simply refused to accept this finding. And after the juiced-up balls somewhat receded as a controversy, a new one arose over 'corked' bats: charges – indeed, at least a couple of actual instances – that players were putting special materials inside their bats to increase their hitting power.

All this, however, was fun and games compared to the more serious flap that arose at the outset of the season – and in an unfortunately ironic way. All of organized baseball, and much of America, was congratualting itself on the fortieth anniversary of Jackie Robinson's joining the Dodgers and thus 'breaking the racial barrier' when, on 8 April, Al Campanis, a Dodgers executive – and as it happens a former teammate and professed friend of Robinson – went on national TV and made some remarks which suggested that blacks didn't quite have the capacity to be managers or executives. In the storm that ensued, Campanis was fired, but the fact is he had unwittingly called attention to an easily ignored situation: organized baseball seemed to have no place for blacks, let alone Hispanics, except on the field. Commissioner Ueberroth quickly insisted he would take steps to see that blacks were given a fair chance at baseball's managerial and executive positions, but as the season came to an end, no blacks had replaced any of the fired managers nor were front offices able to point to any real increase of black personnel. So Jackie Robinson's celebration turned out to be a reminder of just how much remained to be done before baseball and American society were truly integrated.

ABOVE: *Darryl Strawberry joined the Mets in 1983, when he took Rookie of the Year honors. He moved to the Los Angeles Dodgers in 1991 and then joined the Giants during the 1994 season. Although not always living up to expectations, he averaged 26 homers per year – 39 in 1987 alone.*

LEFT: *Don Mattingly, star first baseman of the Yankees since 1982, won the league batting title in 1984 with his .343 average and ranked eighth in the majors in 1987.*

RIGHT: *Tim Raines excels at both baserunning and hitting – he led the National League in stolen bases four times since joining the Expos in 1979 and led the league with his .344 batting average in 1986. In 1987 he led the league in runs (123), stole 50 bases and batted .330. He went to the Chicago White Sox in 1991.*

BELOW: *Wade Boggs, the Red Sox third baseman, has taken the league's batting title four times since 1983, most recently in 1987 with a .363.*

OPPOSITE: *Paul Molitor, with the Brewers from 1978 to 1992 as second or third baseman, had a great season in 1987: he led the league in runs (114) and doubles (41) and was second with his .353 average, and he dominated the sports pages while he ran his hitting streak to 39 consecutive games. In 1993 he joined the Toronto Blue Jays and helped them take the World Series that year.*

BELOW: *Don Baylor, designated hitter extraordinaire, comes crashing into home plate in the seventh and deciding game of the 1987 World Series. Baylor enjoyed the unique experience of joining the Red Sox in 1986 and helping them take the pennant, and then moving to the Twins late in 1987 and going all the way with them against the Cardinals.*

After all this, the season on the field might seem to have been an anticlimax. Not so: it was one of the most tightly contested in recent years, with two division titles being clinched only in the last days of September and the other two races going right up to the wire. In the National League Eastern Division, most students of the game conceded that the Mets should repeat. Instead, the Cardinals moved fairly early into the lead and then the Mets were forced to chase them, with the Expos also on their heels, right to the end. In the Western Division, Cincinnati was picked to win, but although manager Pete Rose did his best

(even declining to activate himself), the San Francisco Giants took first place. In the playoffs, the Cardinals defeated the Giants, four games to three.

In the American League's Eastern Division, even the Red Sox's diehard fans didn't expect them to repeat, but the Yankees were generally regarded as about due to claim first place. But the Yankees never could really pull it all together; instead, the Blue Jays and the Tigers fought it out right to the last day, with the Tigers coming out on top. In the Western Division, some knowledgeable sports commentators had picked the Texas Rangers, but the Minnesota Twins

eventually moved into first place and held on. In the playoffs, the Twins defeated the Tigers, four games to one.

In the 1987 World Series, the more experienced Cardinals were generally favored over the younger Twins, and when the Twins won the first two games in the Metrodome, that was chalked up to homefield advantage. Sure enough, in St Louis the Cardinals took the next three games. But back in the Minneapolis, the Twins won the sixth game easily, 11-5, and then held on to win the seventh game, 4-2, to gain the club's first World Series Championship.

TOP: *Frank Viola, pitching for the Twins, beat the Cardinals in the first and last games of the 1987 World Series and was named Series MVP.*

ABOVE: *Hard-hitting Kirby Puckett, who joined the Twins in 1984, helped his team to their first World Championship in 1987.*

RIGHT: *With his unequalled 59 straight scoreless innings and his 22-8 season record, Cy Young Award winner Orel Hershiser helped the Dodgers win it all in 1988. His stellar post-season performance – including two World Series wins against the A's – earned him MVP honors for both the NLCs and the Fall Classic.*

BELOW: *The Cubs' 72-year tradition of only daytime baseball at home ended on 8 August 1988, when the lights were switched on at Wrigley Field for the first time ever. A capacity crowd and rooftop spectators witnessed the historic Cubs-Phillies night game.*

The 1988 season began relatively peacefully, considering all the scandals and controversies off and on the field that seem to distract fans these days. The one outstanding issue came about from the order to umpires to enforce the balk rule strictly. And indeed, almost from opening day, umpires did begin to call balks – so many that the old record of 356 for the season (for both leagues) was soon wiped out. By the end of the season, called balks were up by 160 percent, yet the predicted worst-case scenario did not materialize: they were so scattered that few of these calls seemed to influence the outcomes of games.

True, team batting averages and home run production were lower than in recent years, and there was the old talk about a new ball being responsible for the change, but cooler students of the game attributed it to better pitching. Tom Browning of the Cincinnati Reds, for one, got himself a perfect game, the 14th in the history of major league baseball, while Orel Hershiser of the Dodgers pitched a record-setting 59 consecutive scoreless innings; with his 22-8 season record, this was good enough to get him the Cy Young Award. Among the other unusual records of 1988 were Jose Canseco's 42 homers *and* 40 stolen bases – the first such pairing in organized baseball – and Don Baylor getting hit by still more pitches to up his total to a new career record of 267.

Other standout events of the 1988 season included Chicago's Wrigley Field finally installing

lights. Oldtimers complained about the end of an era, but the fact was that baseball was more popular than ever. By the end of the season, major league clubs would set a new single-season attendance record for the fourth consecutive year.

When the 1988 season began, experienced sports writers were saying that there would be no surprises this year: clearly the Mets and the Yankees were going all the way, they predicted, with the Giants and the Oakland A's as runners-up. In the National League, instead it was the Pirates and Dodgers who took the early leads in their divisions; by the All-Star break, the Mets had indeed taken over and went on to win the Eastern Division, but the Dodgers held on to win the Western Division. The Mets let down the experts in the playoffs when the Dodgers took four of the seven games and won the pennant.

But this was nothing compared to the surprise that awaited fans over in the American League. In the Western Division, the prophets were right: the A's took an early lead and never looked back. But the Eastern Division was something else. It began with a league record that a team would gladly forego: the Baltimore Orioles lost their first 21 games. By the end of April the Cleveland Indians were in first place, and by the All-Star break the Tigers were there. As for the Yankees, George Steinbrenner did what he always did in such situations: he fired Billy Martin (for the fifth time). The Red Sox also fired their manager, John McNamara, and named their third-base coach, Joe Morgan, as a temporary manager. When the Bosox began to win game after game, Morgan was named permanent manager, and the Sox went on winning – including 24 consecutive games at Fenway Park. On Labor Day they moved into first place; holding off first the Tigers and then the Milwaukee Brewers, the Boston Red Sox won their division after one of the more dramatic turnarounds in recent years.

The American League's miracle ended there, however, for the Oakland A's swept the Red Sox in four straight and then went on to lose to the Dodgers, 4-1, in a Series memorable for the MVP performance of veteran Kirk Gibson. The pundits had been wrong, but the fans were the real winners.

The 1989 season might be dubbed 'The Fissure Season' because it began with the Pete Rose scandal that divided many baseball fans and ended with the earthquake that interrupted the World Series. The former began in March when *Sports Illustrated* carried a story alleging that Pete Rose had bet on baseball games, including some Reds' games when he was their player-manager. Although Rose continued to deny the charges and threatened to challenge the traditional right of the Commissioner to pass judgment on him, there was enough evidence that in August he struck a compromise: the evidence would not be officially exhibited but he would accept the judgment. The new Commissioner (since March), A. Bartlett Giamatti, then suspended Rose for life from any involvement with organized baseball, with the right to appeal this status a year later.

But that was by no means the end of the rumblings. Barely a week after his decision, Giamatti died of a heart attack. Because of his unusual background

LEFT: *In 1988 Jose Canseco became organized baseball's first 40-40 man, with 42 round-trippers and 40 stolen bases. With a league-leading 124 RBIs that year as well, the popular and powerful outfielder was voted the AL MVP.*

ABOVE: *A sure bet for the Hall of Fame until his gambling scandal broke in 1989, Pete Rose was banned from baseball for life by Commissioner A Bartlett Giamatti.*

LEFT: *A's ace reliever Dennis Eckersley led the league in saves with 45 in 1988, helping his team to the first of three consecutive American League championships.*

RIGHT: *Incoming National League president Bill White is congratulated by outgoing NL president and soon-to-be commissioner A Bartlett Giamatti in February 1989.*

BELOW: *Will Clark, one of the Giants' offensive leaders, turned in a career year in 1989. Batting .333 while scoring a league-leading 104 runs, Will the Thrill turned on the afterburners in the post-season. Despite Clark's MVP performance in the NLCS, the Giants were dominated in the World Series by the heavy-hitting A's.*

BELOW RIGHT: *San Francisco's third baseman Matt Williams hit two home runs in the 1989 NLCS and one in the World Series. Together with Will Clark, Robby Thompson, Kevin Mitchell and Brett Butler, Williams was part of the NL's hottest lineup that season.*

– he was a literary scholar, and former president of Yale University – he had brought a new spirit and status to baseball, so his premature passing was a great loss. Francis Fay Vincent, Giamatti's assistant, was immediately elected the new Commissioner. Meanwhile, the split caused by the Rose incident was between those who felt that Rose had lost his chance of being elected to the Baseball Hall of Fame and those who felt that election to the Hall had nothing to do with off-field behavior or morality. When in 1990 Rose was sentenced to five months in jail for cheating on his income taxes, that only hardened the lines; the final blow fell in 1991 when the directors of the Hall of Fame voted to deny entry to anyone ever suspended from baseball – a move clearly designed to prevent Rose's supporters from someday voting him in.

Also during Giamatti's brief tenure, Bill White – former National League star (1956-69) and a well-known sportscaster – was named president of the National League, the first African-American to hold such a position. As to the National League's season on the field, the Eastern Division provided a great upset when the highly favored New York Mets fizzled and the Chicago Cubs actually managed to hold onto first place through the final day. In the Western Division, the Giants, who had let their fans down in 1988, held off the Padres and Astros and came through in 1989. In the NL playoffs, the superior hitting of the Giants' Will Clark, Matt Williams, and Kevin Mitchell dominated the Cubs – the fans' favorite because of the beleaguered club's reputation as the perpetual underdog – and the Giants won, four games to one.

Over in the American League, the Western Division race provided few surprises as the Oakland A's, holding off mild threats from the Kansas City Royals and the California Angels, took first place. The real excitement came in the AL East, where the Toronto Blue Jays had been picked to win; win they did, but only after overtaking the surprisingly feisty Baltimore Orioles in the final weeks and then holding off the Orioles in the last weekend of the season. A subtext to this exciting race was the fact that this was the first time that both teams were managed by African-Americans – the Blue Jays by Cito Gaston, the Orioles by Frank Robinson. In the playoffs the Blue Jays came up against Oakland stars Jose Canseco, Mark McGwire, Rickey Henderson, and Dave Henderson and the A's took the series, four games to one.

When the 1989 World Series began, everyone thought that it would always be remembered as the BART series, a reference to the fact that it was dedicated to 'Bart' Giamatti and that the host cities were linked by the Bay Area Rapid Transit System (BART). The A's took the first two games in Oakland, and the series moved to Candlestick Park. At 8:04 p.m. on 17 October, shortly before the third game was due to start, a major earthquake struck the San Francisco area, and the game was cancelled due to the possibility of structural damage to the stadium, even though no one in the ballpark was injured. There was some debate as to whether the series should even proceed, given the extent of the disaster in the Bay Area, but eventually everyone agreed that baseball, like life, has to pick up and go on, so on 27 October the series was revived. So, too, were the A's, and they went on to win the two games that gave them a sweep.

But if 1989 will be remembered as the season of the earthquake, it should also be remembered as the year that Nolan Ryan posted the all-time career record of 5000 strikeouts – and proceeded with each game to set a record that may well prove to be one of the few 'untouchables' in the future of the game. And

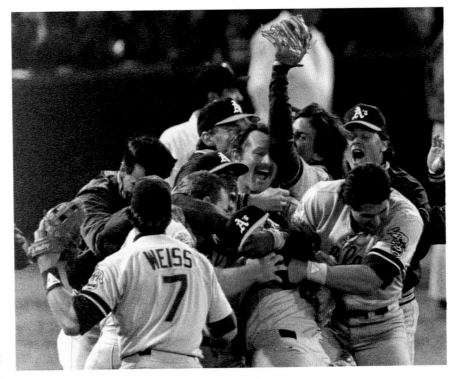

ABOVE: *The Oakland A's celebrate their World Series sweep of the Giants at Candlestick Park in 1989. The final game victory came 11 days after the earthquake that rocked San Francisco and disrupted game three.*

LEFT: *The A's Dave Henderson (right) is congratulated by Mark McGwire after hitting a home run against the Blue Jays in the 1989 ALCS. The A's went on to take the series four games to one.*

FAR LEFT: *Durable pitcher Nolan Ryan set the all-time mark for career strikeouts in 1989, reaching 5000. The Ryan Express retired four years later with 5714 strikeouts and an unprecedented seven no-hitters.*

as the 1980s came to an end, the year 1989 was also widely observed as the 150th anniversary of 'the invention' of baseball by Abner Doubleday in Cooperstown, New York. Although the true story of the evolution of baseball has long since exposed the Doubleday myth, the legend serves a useful function by reminding Americans of the deep-rooted appeal of the game and of the role it continues to play in American life.

CHAPTER NINE
Top of the Order: The 1990s

As the last decade of the 20th century opened, baseball seemed more dynamic than ever, and if major league baseball faced some serious problems – from inflated salaries to drug abuse – it could be argued that this was precisely because baseball was so inextricably interwoven with the total fabric of American life.

Labor disputes, for instance, had become something of an American tradition, so it was not really surprising that the 1990 season began with the owners 'locking out' the players for 32 days at the outset of spring training over a contract dispute; eventually it was settled with a new Basic Agreement that, among other items, raised the minimum salary to $100,000. This was also the year in which the owners were once more found guilty of conspiring to avoid bidding up the salaries of free agents; the owners had to pay the Players Association $280 million and agreed to pay triple damages if ever again found guilty of such collusion. This was the year, too, when George Steinbrenner was forced to withdraw as chief owner and managing director of the Yankees 'for the best interest of baseball' because of a sordid case involving Dave Winfield and a gambler. One might have expected the fans to walk out to protest all these financial shenanigans, but in fact they would turn out at the ballparks in record numbers – including an all-time single season record of over four million in Toronto's new Skydome.

In fact, as soon as the season got going, attention focused where it belonged – on the game. In the National League West, the Cincinnati Reds, without Rose but with a new manager, Lou Piniella, pushed the Dodgers aside to take first place. In the NL East, the Mets were again favored, but this time were toppled by the Pittsburgh Pirates, led by Bobby Bonilla and Barry Bonds – who together accounted for 65 HRs and 235 RBIs – and the Cy Young Award pitching of Doug Drabek. The tables were turned in the playoffs, however, when the favored Pirates lost to the Reds in six games.

In the American League West, the heavily favored A's repeated, leaving the Chicago White Sox nine games behind in second place. The AL East provided some real excitement when the Toronto

OPPOSITE: *After helping the Pirates to three straight division titles, slugging left fielder Barry Bonds signed a five-year contract with the Giants in 1993 worth $46 million. A perpetual Gold Glover and multiple MVP Award winner, Bonds continues to deliver.*

RIGHT: *Pittsburgh's ace Doug Drabek followed his 1990 Cy Young Award-winning year with another trip to the NLCS in 1991. Here he celebrates the division-clinching win in 1991.*

ABOVE: *Billy Hatcher is congratulated after his two-run homer in the third game of the 1990 NLCS. The Reds finished off Pittsburgh in six games, then with Hatcher batting .750, swept the favored A's in the World Series.*

ABOVE RIGHT: *After a year playing in Japan, Cecil Fielder returned to blast 51 home runs for the Tigers in 1990. He led the league in homers again the following year, with 44.*

RIGHT: *With the White Sox in 1990, fireman Bobby Thigpen set a single-season record of 57 saves, posting a stingy 1.83 ERA.*

Blue Jays, also picked to repeat, blew their lead with only eight games left and the Boston Red Sox came out in first place. When the A's swept Boston four straight in the playoffs, the media began to hype another 'unstoppable dynasty,' but in one of the biggest upsets in recent World Series history, Oakland fell in four straight games to Cincinnati, led by Billy Hatcher's all-time Series record .750 BA. Others who had outstanding seasons were Dennis Eckersley, with an 0.61 ERA and 48 saves (second all-time high); Cecil Fielder, with 51 home runs for Detroit after returning from a season in Japan; and Bobby Thigpen, whose 77 appearances as a reliever set a new AL record.

The 1991 season began relatively free of any controversies, off- or on-field, thus allowing total concentration on the game itself. In the National League East the Pittsburgh Pirates once again dominated, but the NL West provided more than its share of surprises. At the All-Star break, the Dodgers were comfortably in first place, and the Atlanta Braves – last-place finishers in their division in the previous three seasons – were nine and a half games behind. But the Braves – sparked by the hitting of Terry Pendleton and Ron Gant and the pitching of Tom Glavine and Steve Avery – hung in there, and by winning their last eight games they pushed the Dodgers out of first on the second-to-last day of the season. Everyone assumed that the Braves had 'peaked' and would be no match for the Pirates, but in an exciting seven-game playoff, Atlanta emerged as the league champions.

The American League proved equally exciting. In the Eastern Division, the Red Sox began as the favorites as they set off with an 18-9 record. Eventually they gave way to the Blue Jays, and despite an epic dash near the end – winning 31 of 41 games in

August-September – they collapsed at the end and settled back into a second-place tie with Detroit, leaving the Blue Jays securely in first with a seven-game lead. In the AL West, it was assumed that the Oakland A's would make it 'no contest,' but instead practically every team in the division held first place for at least a day. It eventually settled down to a two-way race between the White Sox and the Twins, with the Twins winning handily eight games ahead. In the playoffs, the Jays took the second game in the Metrodome – the first that the Twins had lost there in post-season play – but then lost the next three, making the Twins the AL champions.

For the first time in baseball history, two teams that had finished in last place in their divisions the year before – the Twins and Braves – were to square off in the World Series. The Twins – with older players, recent experience in the Series, and the home field advantage of five games in the Metrodome – were widely favored over the enthusiastic but inexperienced Braves. The Twins did indeed take the first two at home, but the Braves took the next three at Atlanta. Back in the Metrodome, it wasn't until Kirby Puckett's homer in the bottom of the 11th that the Twins won the sixth game. In the seventh game, the teams played nine scoreless innings, and only in the bottom of the 10th did the Twins get a run across to become World Champions in one of the most exciting Series in recent years.

The year 1991 was also memorable as the year that Rickey Henderson took over the all-time base-stealing record, and that 44-year-old Nolan Ryan got his record-setting seventh no-hitter. And when the National League announced that it had awarded two new franchises – to Denver and Miami – it was proof that major league baseball was still expanding, still engaging, and still very much the national pastime.

RIGHT: *Explosive on the basepaths, Rickey Henderson beat Lou Brock's record to become the all-time base-stealing leader in 1991. His 130 thefts in 1982 is still the single-season benchmark.*

BELOW: *Sharing the NL lead with 20 wins in 1992, Greg Maddux won the first of an unprecedented three consecutive Cy Young Awards – the first with the Cubs, the second two with the Braves.*

OPPOSITE: *Tom Glavine contributed 20 wins in both 1991 and 1992 to a team whose formidable pitching lineup also featured John Smoltz and Steve Avery. The Atlanta Braves were NL champs both seasons.*

The 1992 season would be the first time that a team from outside the United States – the Toronto Blue Jays – would contend for baseball's world championship. In another landmark, the $28 million awarded Bobby Bonilla when he moved from the Pirates to the Mets set a new contract record – until Cal Ripken, with 1,735 consecutive games, was awarded $30.5 million.

In off-the-field news, Commissioner Fay Vincent was dismissed by the major league club owners when he insisted on placing the Chicago Cubs in the Western Division to accommodate the Colorado Rockies and the Florida Marlins, the National League's two new franchises for 1993. Milwaukee Brewers owner 'Bud' Selig assumed interim chairmanship. In the middle of the World Series, veteran announcer Red Barber, who had announced the first major league night game and the first televised game, died at the age of 84.

Although at the season's outset the Mets were favored in the National League, the Pittsburgh Pirates held the lead for all but 10 days that season, successfully fending off the Montreal Expos into September to take their third straight Eastern Division title. The Atlanta Braves, despite their highly-touted pitching staff, wavered until after the All-Star break, when they overtook the Reds and finally the Padres to secure their second consecutive Western Division title just two days after the Pirates clinched their division on 27 September.

Facing the Braves in the league championship for the second consecutive year, the Pirates were the pick of the sportswriters. The Braves took a three-to-one lead, and Pittsburgh took the next two games to even up the series. In the seventh game the Pirates held a 2-0 lead until the bottom of the ninth. Then Atlanta's Terry Pendleton scored on a sacrifice fly and pinch hitter Francisco Cabrera, with only 10 major league at-bats that season, drove in David Justice and Sid Bream with a two-out single to give Atlanta its second consecutive pennant.

With 34 homers and 39 steals, Pittsburgh's MVP Barry Bonds logged his second 30-30 year to become one of only five players – including his father, Bobby – ever to have achieved this feat. The Cubs' Greg Maddux took Cy Young honors for the second time. Pitching phenom Nolan Ryan took his career strike-out blitz to a total of 5,668. And on 20 September, Philadelphia's Mickey Morandi scored the National League's fourth unassisted triple play – the ninth in major league history.

In the American League, the Twins lost their lead after the All-Star break to an Oakland club that overcame early-season injuries to clinch the Western Division on 28 September. The Blue Jays, strengthened by veteran slugger Dave Winfield and their first 20-game-winning pitcher, Jack Morris, occupied first place in the East by mid-season. After fighting off Baltimore and Milwaukee, they clinched their second consecutive divisional title on 3 October.

Oakland took the first league championship game, dropped the next three, and won the fifth. By winning the sixth game, 9-2, the Jays became the first team from outside the United States ever to win

ABOVE: *Blue Jays fans celebrate Toronto's historic World Series win over the Braves in 1992 after watching the game played in Atlanta on the Skydome's giant scoreboard.*

RIGHT: *Joe Carter is congratulated by Toronto teammates after his solo home run in game three of the 1992 World Series. Of Carter's six Series hits, two were doubles and two were homers.*

a pennant. Their skipper, Cito Gaston, became the first African-American ever to manage a team into the World Series. Also that season, George Brett and Robin Yount logged their 3000th hits, and Jeff Reardon became the all-time relief leader. Dave Winfield, at age 40, became the oldest man ever to hit 100 RBIs (108). Oakland's Dennis Eckersley took the American League's MVP and Cy Young awards.

In the World Series, the Braves won the first game, and after the US Marines color guard accidentally flew the Canadian flag upside-down, Toronto took the next three. A grand slam from Atlanta's Lonnie Smith in the Skydome gave the Braves game five and moved the Series back to Atlanta. There the Jays survived a gruelling four-hour-plus game until Dave Winfield's 11th-inning hit – his first ever extra-base hit in a Series – made Toronto the first non-American team ever to win the World Series in only their 16th season as a club.

Before the 1993 season began, the major league club owners made news by refusing to name a commissioner to replace the deposed Fay Vincent. Milwaukee's 'Bud' Selig remained in place as interim chairman. Meanwhile, George Steinbrenner was allowed to return to take full command of the Yankees. In February 1993, the owners voted to ban Marge Schott, owner of the Cincinnati Reds, for one year and fined her $25,000 for using 'ethnic slurs'. Still, the debut of the Colorado Rockies and the Florida Marlins, the first new clubs added to the major leagues since the Montreal Expos and the San Diego Padres in 1969, promised to make the National League particularly interesting.

The American League season got underway with no clear-cut front runners. Toronto had let several

of its key players go, causing many sportswriters to pick the Orioles in the Eastern Division. Yet Toronto, although briefly bumped out of first place by the Red Sox and the Yankees, proved dominant, as for the first time for any team this century, their top three hitters were also the league's three best hitters: John Olerud (.363), Paul Molitor (.332), and Roberto Alomar (.326). In the West, the White Sox moved into first place quickly and were never seriously threatened.

Chalking up their second pennant in as many years, the Blue Jays took the league championship from the White Sox in six games. White Sox pitcher Jack McDowell received the American League's Cy Young Award, and teammate Frank Thomas was named MVP. In other American League landmarks, Nolan Ryan, George Brett, and Carleton Fisk all ended their major league careers – Fisk with the career record for most games caught at 2,226. The ageless Dave Winfield, now with the Minnesota

BELOW LEFT: *White Sox ace 'Black Jack' McDowell took Cy Young Award honors in 1993, when he posted top figures in wins and shutouts. Difficult to steal against, the 6'5" right-hander presents an imposing figure on the mound.*

BELOW: *Frank Thomas adds a home run to Chicago's winning cause in the sixth game of the 1993 ALCS. The power-hitting first baseman was instrumental in the White Sox's division title that year.*

Twins, became the 19th major league player to log 3,000 hits. Seattle hurler Chris Bosio managed a no-hitter, as did the Yankees' Jim Abbott, an especially admirable feat for a pitcher with only one hand.

In the National League East the Phillies moved into first place at the beginning of the season and stayed there despite threats from the Cardinals and the Expos. The hapless Mets fell into last place with the worst winning percentage in the majors – .364 – to finish behind even the rookie Florida Marlins.

In the National League West the San Francisco Giants, with their new acquisition Barry Bonds, took a surprisingly strong lead and by August were 10 games up on the second-place Braves. As Bonds briefly slumped, however, Atlanta moved up, and at the end of the season both teams were tied for first with 103 wins each. In the final games of the season, the Giants lost to the Dodgers, and the Braves, facing

the Colorado Rockies, surmounted them easily to secure their third divisional title in a row.

Favored by experience in the league championship series, the Braves indeed out-hit and out-scored the rough-hewn Phillies over six games. But the Phillies, by getting the extra runs when they counted, mimicked Atlanta's 1991 miracle and jumped from finishing at the bottom of their division the previous year to winning the pennant.

Barry Bonds and Greg Maddux, now both with different teams, repeated as the National League's MVP and Cy Young award winners. Darryl Kite of the Astros pitched a no-hitter, and Mark Whiten of the Cardinals hit four homers and drove in 12 runs in a single game, tying two major league records in one of the most productive days on record. The rookie Colorado Rockies shattered all previous season attendance figures with 4,483,350 tickets sold. Both

OPPOSITE: *The Yankees' Jim Abbott unleashes a pitch in the eighth inning of his no-hitter vs. the Indians at Yankee Stadium on 4 September 1993.*

BELOW LEFT: *Lenny Dykstra watches his home run soar in game four of the 1993 World Series. The offensive sparkplug led the colorful Phillies' onslaught in the regular season as well, leading the NL in hits, runs and walks that year.*

BELOW: *The Blue Jays' outstanding DH Paul Molitor connects for a solo round-tripper in game six of the 1993 World Series. Toronto went on to win the Series for their second consecutive World Championship.*

BELOW RIGHT: *A fixture in Baltimore, stalwart Cal Ripken, Jr. readies himself at shortstop. If he stays healthy, Ripken could surpass Lou Gehrig's consecutive-game mark in 1996.*

OPPOSITE: *Ken Griffey, Jr. continues to prove his worth to the Mariners. On his way to drilling 45 home runs in 1993, Griffey homered in eight consecutive games, tying a major league record. He was on track to break Roger Maris's home run record, leading the league in homers, when the 1994 strike season ended in August. Superb on defense as well, the center fielder is a perpetual Gold Glove winner.*

new clubs, the Rockies and the Marlins, avoided finishing last in their divisions. Amidst talk of a general decline in pitching skills, home runs were up a whopping 55 percent over 1992 in the Senior Circuit (and 16.8 percent in the American League).

In what would prove to be an exciting World Series matchup, Canada's defending champions took the first game of the Series, 8-5, but the Phillies, thanks to a three-run homer from Jim Eisenreich, took the second, 6-4. Moving to Philadelphia, the Jays took the third, 10-3. The fourth game, lasting an incredible 4 hours and 14 minutes before it fell to Toronto, 15-14, was not only the longest postseason game in major league history but, with its total of 29 runs, 31 hits and no errors, the highest-scoring postseason game in major league history.

Miraculously, the Phillies regrouped to shut out the Jays, 2-0. Then the action returned to Toronto, where the Phillies looked like they might tie up the Series in game six until, in the bottom of the ninth, Joe Carter hit one over the fence off Mitch 'Wild Thing' Williams. This was only the second time in baseball history that a player had won a Series with a home run (Bill Mazeroski did it in 1960). Toronto's 8-6 win made it the first club to win back-to-back world championships since the 1977-1978 Yankees.

The 1994 season began with a new three-division-per-league structure that realigned some traditional rivalries, but more controversially provided for the best second-place team from each league to become the fourth team in the playoffs. Such a 'wild

card' team would face the first-place team with the best record and could, by winning a short series, end up in the World Series – and even win that. What would standings mean?

This question was never to be answered, because the season, which also began with the threat of a strike, came to a screeching halt. Baseball had seen seven other work stoppages since 1972, but the strike of 1994, the first mid-season walkout since 1985, was the first time that a labor dispute actually ended a season. It was also the first time since 1904 that the World Series – played through two world wars – was not played.

As for the new divisional lineups, beginning in 1994 the National League East included the Atlanta Braves, the Philadelphia Phillies, the Montreal Expos, the Florida Marlins, and the New York Mets. The National League West included the San Francisco Giants, the Los Angeles Dodgers, the Colorado Rockies, and the San Diego Padres. The new National League Central Division included the St Louis Cardinals, the Houston Astros, the Chicago Cubs, the Pittsburgh Pirates, and the Cincinnati Reds.

In the American League, the revamped Eastern Division included the Baltimore Orioles, the Boston Red Sox, the Detroit Tigers, the New York Yankees, and the Toronto Blue Jays. The American League West included the California Angels, the Oakland Athletics, the Seattle Mariners, and the Texas Rangers. The new American League Central Divi-

sion included the Chicago White Sox, the Cleveland Indians, the Kansas City Royals, the Milwaukee Brewers, and the Minnesota Twins.

The Braves were picked in the National League East to top their division for the fourth consecutive year, but by the All-Star break the Expos had moved one game ahead of Atlanta. In the National League West, despite predictions of a race between San Francisco and Los Angeles, the upstart Rockies, in their second season, took second place behind the Dodgers. In the new Central Division, at the All-Star break the Reds held a two-and-a-half game lead over the Astros.

In the second half of the season the Expos, with the second lowest payroll in the majors, expanded their lead over the Braves to six games. The Giants displaced the Rockies behind the Dodgers, and Houston moved to only half a game behind the Reds. Attendance looked like it would break records in both leagues, and it was a truly exciting season. Matt Williams hit home runs at a pace that threatened Roger Maris' home run record.

In the American League East the Blue Jays, picked to take their third consecutive divisional title, fell behind the Yankees and the Orioles. In the American League West, the Rangers held a five-game lead over second-place Seattle in a tight division race. As for the new Central Division, by the All-Star break the Indians, who had not been in a post-season game in 40 years, were tied with the favored White Sox.

As the second half of the season began, the Yankees widened their lead over the Orioles to six-and-a-half games; Oakland moved one game behind the Rangers; and Chicago held a one-game lead over Cleveland. Rangers and Indians fans enjoyed

their new ballparks, and many stars were enjoying big years: Kenny Rogers of the Rangers had a perfect game, Boston's John Valentin made an un-assisted triple play, and Ken Griffey Jr of Seattle joined Matt Williams' assault on the season home run record.

When the strike began on August 12, at first neither side was prepared to negotiate. Last-minute efforts in September failed, and on September 14 'acting commissioner' Bud Selig, owner of the Brewers, announced that the major league baseball season was officially over.

The heart of the matter was the owners' insistence on a salary cap for players. The owners argued that teams from smaller markets did not receive enough revenue from local TV and other sources to compete on an even footing with teams from major markets, but the players saw this as a thinly disguised way to limit their salaries and to avoid getting their own houses in order.

Indeed, the owners seemed to have a lot to answer for by not choosing a new commissioner for the third consecutive season. Selig, himself a team owner, was hardly in a position to order players and owners to get back on the field and play ball 'for the good of the game.'

Not since the Black Sox scandal of 1919 had the national pastime given its fans so much to be disenchanted about. The season ended with Greg Maddux looking for an elusive third consecutive Cy Young Award (which he won); Barry Bonds reaching for his fourth MVP (which he didn't win); and Tony Gwynn, with an astonishing .394 batting average, threatening to become the first player since Ted Williams to average .400. In the season that never was, we will never know what might have been.

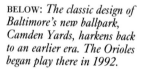

BELOW: *The classic design of Baltimore's new ballpark, Camden Yards, harkens back to an earlier era. The Orioles began play there in 1992.*

Index